AN AVERAGE PILOT

THE STORY OF A
WORLD WAR II SWORDFISH NIGHT MISSION
OVER THE STRAIT OF SICILY

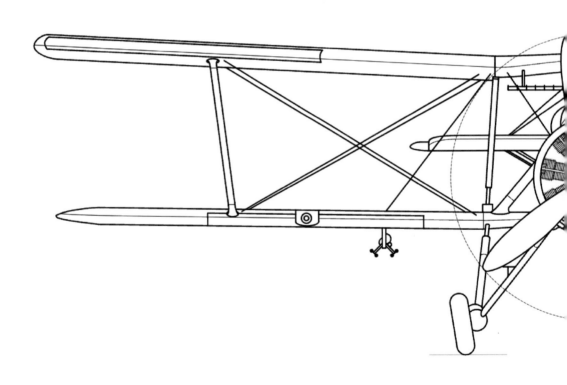

AN AVERAGE PILOT

THE STORY OF A
WORLD WAR II SWORDFISH NIGHT MISSION
OVER THE STRAIT OF SICILY

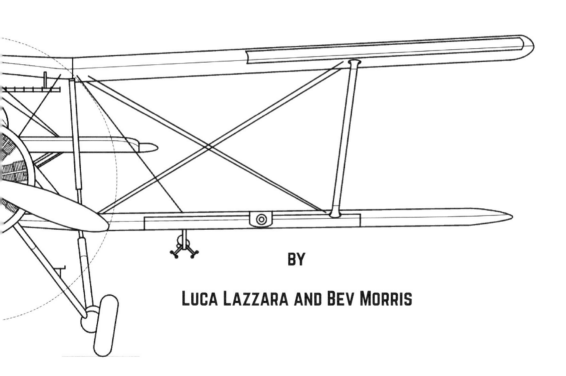

BY

LUCA LAZZARA AND BEV MORRIS

DOUBLE‡DAGGER

Library and Archives Canada Cataloguing in Publication
Lazzara, Luca author
Morris, Bev author
An Average Pilot / Luca Lazzara and Bev Morris

Issued in print and electronic formats.
ISBN: 978-1-990644-67-2 (soft cover)
ISBN: 978-1-990644-68-9 (e-pub)
ISBN: 978-1-990644-69-6 (Kindle)

Editor: Phil Halton
Cover design: Pablo Javier Herrera
Interior design: Winston A. Prescott

Cover Image: Fairey Swordfish K8405 on the beach at Cefalù, Sicily, 12 November 1941. (Martino & Marino Families)

Double Dagger Books Ltd
Toronto, Ontario, Canada
www.doubledagger.ca

TABLE OF CONTENTS

PROLOGUE

MILITARY HISTORIES DO NOT HAVE A BEGINNING or an end, more a series of connections that resonate through the present and into the future. This story, of a Royal Navy Fleet Air Arm mission over the Strait of Sicily on the night of 11 November 1941, is one of many, many similar tales of skill and determination that have not always been told. It did not start out as a book, just as one airline captain's interest in how a Fairey Swordfish aircraft landed, upside-down, on the beach he remembered from his childhood. It soon became a global search for aircrew, their families and the fragments of history that would piece together the story of "an average pilot" and the crew of the Swordfish mission.

Captain Luca Lazzara, intrigued by a faded black and white photograph of the capsized Swordfish, followed his curiosity across history and nations, contacting military historians, serving personnel, and the families and friends of the aircrew. He amassed primary evidence, secondary sources, and anecdotes to provide insight into how a pilot could execute such an unorthodox landing.

Luca then approached Dr. Bev Morris to write this book with him and to stitch together the facts and the possibilities of what happened that night, to bring alive a story of fortitude and resilience that the aircrew of 830 Squadron embodied. She embarked on research into the mission and the Swordfish, affectionately known as the "Stringbag," and discovered the character of an aircraft that endeared itself to pilots and aircrew. Using the voices and memories of soldiers and pilots from 830 Squadron, as well as written accounts of the mission, she has reimagined the conversations in the cockpit and the feelings of that night and has woven these in with the known technical details and historical facts from the era.

Together, Luca and Bev have reflected on what might have happened that night, driven by their desire to uncover the true story and their determination to keep the stories alive that are important to all of us in this uncertain world.

Now, we want you to decide if there is really "an average pilot" in these pages, imagine their journey, and to help us trace the remaining family members.

Opposite: Detail of "Swordfish" by Chas McHugh.

i

Acknowledgments

PEOPLE IN THE MILITARY FAMILY HAVE BIG HEARTS and many of them have given their time and resources generously and freely throughout our research. We would like to thank them all for helping us to trace the story of this mission and to find the ancestors of the men who flew it.

All the families of the crew who provided us with insight into the sort of men their fathers were and who shared family documents and memories to help us bring to life the story deserve our thanks. In particular, we'd like to thank Sally Ogilvie (daughter of Raymond Taylor) and her brother John Taylor, Chris Fallon (son of Johnny Fallon) and Ian Campbell (son of Stewart Campbell), Angela Griffiths (aunt of Ken Griffiths), David Engerran (grandson of John Hunt), Jennifer Wigram (daughter-in-law of Aidan Wigram) and Duncan Lawson (son of Bobby Lawson).

Phil Glover, a retired Aircraft Engineer officer of the Royal Navy Fleet Air Arm, has been incredibly helpful by sharing his own research and insights into the individual men and the operations of 830 Squadron. Phil's support has been invaluable to provide us with information about the fate of the men after leaving the military as well as checking details of the communications and standard operating procedures used during the mission.

The academic research and conservation work of Professor Gianfranco Purpura (University of Palermo, retired), Tullio Marcon (former Italian Navy engineer and expert on military history) and Ray Polidano at the Malta Aviation Museum have been critical in documenting the history around Sicily and Malta which enabled the wrecks to be located.

The catalyst for this book was an image posted by Serge Rajmondi, creator of the Facebook group "Foto Storiche Cefalù." We would like to thank him and the Martino and Marino families for sharing the photographs that inspired this book.

Also, thanks to Nina Pearson at the Fleet Air Arm and the volunteer historians, Lee Howard, Tim Brown and Nick Blackman OBE, who provided us with details about mission callsigns, communications, and aircraft identification numbers. Finally, thank you to Sarah Wragg who gave her time to provide feedback on our early manuscript and to encourage us to make this book a reality.

Opposite: The seaside looking from Cefalù towards the Swordfish K8405 crash site. (Lazzara, 2020)

SINGLE-ENGINE AIRCRAFT				MULTI-ENGINE AIRCRAFT							PASS-ENGER	INSTR. FLYING cols. (1
DAY		NIGHT		DAY			NIGHT					
	PILOT	DUAL	PILOT	DUAL	1ST PILOT	2ND PILOT	DUAL	1ST PILOT	2ND PILOT			DUAL
(1)	(2)	(3)	(4)	(5)	(6)	(7)	(8)	(9)	(10)		(11)	(12)
.20	46.45	2.45	0.25								0.10	9.10
.50												.50

(*1752) Wt. 10744—262 4,000 5/36 T.S. **667**

FORM 414

SUMMARY of FLYING and ASSESSMENTS FOR ~~YEAR~~ *TERM* COMMENCING 1st 22 — 1 — *19

[* For Officer, insert "JUNE" ; For Airman Pilot, insert "AUGUST."]

	S.E. AIRCRAFT		M.E. AIRCRAFT		TOTAL
	Day	Night	Day	Night	
DUAL	25.50	2.45			28.35
PILOT	23.25	0.25			23.50
PASSENGER	—	—	—	—	

TERM GRAND TOTAL
52 Hrs. **25** M
(Excluding Passenger)

ASSESSMENT of ABILITY

(To be assessed as :—Exceptional, Above the Average, Average, or Below the Average)

(i)   AS A Pop14 PILOT ...... *Average*

(ii) AS PILOT–NAVIGATOR/NAVIGATOR ... *Average*

(iii) IN BOMBING

(iv) IN AIR GUNNERY ......

† Insert :—" F.", " L.B.", " G.R.", " F.B.", etc.

ANY POINTS IN FLYING OR AIRMANSHIP WHICH SHOULD BE WATCHED.

Date   5. 4. 40

Signature ......
Chief Flying Instructor.
Officer Commanding ...... No. 1 F.T.S. Netheravon

0	46.45	2.45	0.25								0.10	10.00
	(2)	(3)	(4)	(5)	(6)	(7)	(8)	(9)	(10)		(11)	(12)

1

THE NIGHT OF THE SWORDFISH

"HOW ARE WE DOING, FRANK?"

"Can't get a proper fix on where we are, Clog. Working on it." Frank Robinson's words, spoken with a lively London accent, were distorted by the Gosport Tubes he spoke through and did little to reassure Raymond "Clog" Taylor. The foul weather, the spotty radio signal, and the growling in his stomach were the least of his worries. They were flying on reserve fuel and running on the last of their luck, somewhere along the Strait of Sicily. Robinson was a good man to have in the sky with you, but even he couldn't see in the dark.

"Osborn seems to know where he's going," said Taylor, nodding towards the aircraft ahead of them. His voice was tight against the drone of the Swordfish, the bitter cold of the night air nipping at his face and drilling into his bones. He was still able to discern the familiar outline of the other three planes flying around him in close formation through the dense clouds. There weren't as many of them as there should have been. Three aircraft had already turned back, one after the other, with mechanical problems. "Malta or bust, eh?"

"I bloody well hope so," Robinson replied. "How are we going to celebrate your birthday up here with no ladies for company, and no beer? A good knees-up is what every chap deserves when he reaches the illustrious age of twenty-three."

"Plenty of time for celebrations when we get back. Good job the old Stringbag's enjoying the trip out, isn't she," Taylor shouted, slapping his hand on the Swordfish's rudimentary instrument panel. "You love it, don't you girl?"

"She might be having fun," Robinson said, "but there's more fun to be had back in the mess with a copy of the National Geographic and a roaring fire."

"Still thinking you'll head to Australia after this is all over?" Taylor asked, hunching further down into the meagre warmth of the sheepskin collar on his flying jacket. It smelled of oil, cigarettes and Tabarome aftershave. Apparently,

Opposite: Sub-Lieutenant Raymond "Clog" Taylor: Logbook entry, 5 April 1940.

Churchill wore it. Not that Taylor had met Churchill, but he liked the connection.

"Ah, the land of kangaroos and crystal blue seas," Robinson mused. "Beats Wandsworth on a rainy Sunday afternoon." Robinson started humming a jolly tune, making Taylor smile. It would have been an amiable night out in better circumstances.

"How long have we been away from base?" Taylor asked, looking for confirmation of what he could see on his own dials.

"Four hours, thirteen minutes," Robinson replied. "We could still make it to Hal Far."

"Osborn seems to have other plans," Taylor said. "We're turning back towards Sicily."

"Interesting choice."

Taylor turned the Stringbag around to follow Osborn. The aircraft might have looked old and cumbersome, but she was reliable and responsive to handle. Taylor appreciated the dependable nature of all the Swordfish in the squadron, but he had a particular soft spot for this one—K8405. He couldn't say why.

Their new course set, the two men flew in silence for a while, catching glimpses of land below them, solid black coast against charcoal-grey sea, elusive through the persistent cloud cover. It was a good night not to be spotted from the ground and a bad night to get lost.

"Can't work out why old Osborn isn't putting us down," Taylor said.

"That man has the gift," Robinson said. "Like one of those music hall magicians. He'll have a trick up his sleeve. Probably a bunch of flowers or some knotted handkerchiefs that go on forever."

"Or maybe it's the ASV radar he's got on board tonight," Taylor said, rubbing his gloved hand across his goggles to remove the ever-present moisture from flying through clouds. "He might know something we don't."

A light flashed from Osborn's aircraft. Taylor and Robinson looked across to see a series of familiar flashes and hand signals, indicating that Osborn was moving into position to land.

"It seems we're going down after all," Taylor said, looking at the fuel gauge. "Can't come too soon for my liking."

"Here's to happy landings," Robinson said, starting to whistle, *We're going to hang out the washing on the Siegfried Line.*

"Here's to any bloody landing," Taylor said to himself.

The four Swordfish moved into their well-rehearsed formation for descent, the mesmerising darkness pulling them forwards, towards the shadows beneath them.

OPPOSITE: Sub-Lieutenant Raymond "Clog" Taylor. (Taylor Family)

Mission Crew and Swordfish designations

Aircraft	Crew member	Role	Place of birth	Date of birth
V4295	Lieutenant George Myles Osborn	Pilot	St. Ann's, Lancashire	15 December, 1914
	Lieutenant-Commander John Gunthorpe Hunt	Commanding Officer, Senior Observer (Navigator)	Hawkhurst, Kent	18 April, 1906
	Sergeant Matthew Parke	RAF Radar Operator	Strabane, Co Tyrone, Northern Ireland	23 May, 1920
K8405	Sub-Lieutenant Raymond Warren Taylor	Pilot	Newport, Wales	11 November, 1918
	Sub-Lieutenant Frank Leonard Robinson	Observer (Backup Navigator)	Wandsworth, London	19 September, 1920
V4421	Sub-Lieutenant Stewart Campbell	Pilot	Southend, Essex	19 May, 1921
	Leading Airman Johnny Fallon	Telegraphist Air Gunner (TAG)	Ashton on Makerfield, Lancashire	20 January, 1920
K5979	Lieutenant Aidan Frederick Wigram	Pilot	Thandiani, Pakistan, North West Frontier	27 May, 1907
	Leading Airman Ken Dickens Griffiths	Telegraphist Air Gunner (TAG)	Salford, Greater Manchester	4 December, 1919

2
THE STRINGBAG

ON THE NIGHT OF 11 NOVEMBER 1941, seven Fairey Swordfish torpedo bombers and a Wellington bomber from 830 Squadron, of the British Royal Navy's Fleet Air Arm, set out from Hal Far air station in Malta.

Four aircraft didn't make it home: these are the Swordfish of this story. Their mission was to disrupt the Axis supply lines through the Strait of Sicily, something they had been doing with increasing regularity.

V4295 was piloted by Lieutenant George Myles "Woozle" Osborn who was joined by two other crew: Lieutenant-Commander John Gunthorpe Hunt acting as Senior Observer (Navigator) and Sergeant Matthew Parke who was an RAF Radar Operator. With three men on board, this was the crew with most experience and was the lead aircraft.

K8405 was piloted by Lieutenant Raymond Warren "Clog" Taylor with Sub-Lieutenant Frank Leonard Robinson flying as Observer. They were an unlikely pairing, with Taylor from a busy seaport in Monmouthshire and Robinson from Wandsworth, a key site for munitions manufacturing in London.

The third plane, V4421, was piloted by Sub-Lieutenant Stewart Campbell with Leading Airman Johnny Fallon as Telegraphist Air Gunner (TAG). Campbell and Fallon were the youngest crew in the mission.

The last aircraft was K5979, piloted by Lieutenant Aidan Frederick Wigram whose TAG that night was Leading Airmen Ken Dickens Griffiths. Again, the men were from very different backgrounds, with Wigram born overseas and Griffiths coming from a depressed area of north-west England.

Pilots talked affectionately about the Swordfish, a biplane torpedo bomber developed by the Fairey Aviation Company in the early 1930s with the internal designation of TSR I – Torpedo-Spotter-Reconnaissance I. Designed by Marcel Lobelle, Swordfish were created to meet a combined set of needs specified by the Admiralty:

"reconnaissance, at sea and over the land; shadowing, by day and night; "spotting" the fall of shot from ship's guns; convoy escort duties such as anti-submarine searches and attack; torpedo and divebombing attacks against shipping, minelaying – and the carrying other heavy loads – which in the Second World War varied from searchlights to rockets, plus depth-charges, bombs and flares." (Lamb 2001:40)

The production of the plane was simplified by its uncomplicated structure, made up of wings constructed of steel spars, a steel-tube fuselage and a fabric covering, hence its nickname, "Stringbag." Another explanation, found in Lamb's *War in the Stringbag* is that some wag remarked that "No housewife on a shopping spree could cram a wider variety of articles into her stringbag." Wherever the name came from, the Stringbag was a big beast with a wingspan of 45 ft 6in, a length of 35 ft 8 in and a height of 12 ft 4 in, with the added trick of folding wings, making it easier to transport on aircraft carriers. Its defensive firepower was limited to one fixed forward firing .303 calibre Vickers machine gun and one rear cockpit flexible .303 calibre Lewis machine gun. With a little imagination and engineering jiggery-pokery, bombs were added to enhance the original design. The most devastating weapon it carried was the aerial torpedo, weighing in at 1610 lb and capable of sinking a 10,000-tonne ship. It took skill to deliver a weapon like this and pilots learned to attack from a steep dive, at speeds of 180 knots pushing 200 knots in extremis. The problem being that at that speed and angle of descent, the wings

ABOVE: A Fairey Swordfish in Flight, No 1 Naval Air Gunnery School (LAC).

might fold back unexpectedly, something best avoided.

The Swordfish was powered by a Bristol Pegasus engine, which was a British nine-cylinder, single row, air-cooled radial aero engine from a fine pedigree of British designed aircraft engines, theoretically giving it a top speed of 154 mph "downhill," as some pilots reported. Clearly, the pilots went beyond this. Yet, despite its size, relatively slow speeds, and the fact that it was supposed to be obsolete, pilots described it as easy to handle because it was high-performing and reliable under sustained pressure: exactly what a pilot in a combat situation needed.

The Swordfish themselves were an anomaly. With their frighteningly basic structure, and what should have been an outdated operational capability, they became the workhorses of the squadron. Originally designed without any luxuries, like a canopy to protect the crew of two or three from the elements, this ensured they could be easily repaired. Their simple design also allowed them to be easily modified, and so as communications technology changed, the Stringbags were upgraded. One of the effective but simple pieces of equipment they received were Gosport Tubes, which offered a rudimentary means of communications between the men inside the aircraft. The tubes had been designed by Parker and Smith-Barry in 1917 to enable instructors to communicate with trainee pilots. Until that point, all communication had been limited to hand signals and shouts. Their design is simple: think of a stethoscope with tubes going directly from the "ears" of a flying helmet to a funnel that acted as a mouthpiece. It was particularly effective as it was able to cut out the noise of the aircraft in flight. As Smith-Barry observes somewhat wryly in his training manual of 1917:

> For dual control, speaking tubes are now being fitted (the Gosport Tube). Up to now it has been necessary to stall the machine to make a momentary conversation possible. This has, however, given a useful indication of the state of the pupil's nerve, as those who are unlikely to prove suitable for scouts generally cling to the side with an unintelligent expression, instead of conversing fluently and with confidence.

This nerve, so apparent in those early aviators, was still abundant in the pilots of the Second World War.

Malta itself, although tactically critical for running supplies to Gibraltar and on to Alexandria, had not been the intended home for a squadron of Swordfish. It lacked the spare parts and maintenance crews needed to transform what had been a Deck Landing Training unit from HMS Argus into a bomber squadron and to keep a squadron of aircraft constantly airworthy. The Royal Navy had little air cover after France capitulated in May 1940 as it had been their role to protect the Mediterranean. Most British aircraft were in use to protect Britain itself and the aircraft were relatively old. With a vast stretch of water to defend and limited resources, it made good sense to use the "odds and sods" of aircraft and personnel available. 830 Royal Naval Air Station (RNAS) was formed by renumbering 767 RNAS and pulling in crew from other squadrons such as 825 Squadron. Taylor himself had served with 825 Squadron in early 1941, where he'd flown with "Bobby" Lawson who would go on to play a critical role in the sinking of the Bismarck.

The aircrew of 830 Squadron found themselves setting up camp on the edge of the Royal Naval Air Station Hal Far airstrip in Malta with the express task of impeding enemy supply lines at sea. Their training aircraft needed to become torpedo bombers, and they needed to operate at night. Everything from bomb racks to night-flying instrument panels had to be sourced, fitted, and maintained by employing considerable ingenuity and a relentless engineering schedule. The black paintwork of the Stringbags of 830 Squadron had a depth to it that absorbed the sky as it flew. Standing next to them, you could sense their raw, muscular power.

In early 1941, merchant ships supplying Rommel in North Africa had been located west of the island of Pantelleria. Their route across the Mediterranean provided an opportunity for the Fleet Air Arm to do serious damage. These

ABOVE: 825 Squadron on HMS Furious, Feb-Apr 1941. Raymond 'Clog' Taylor (middle row, 1st from the right). Robert 'Bobby' Lawson (3rd middle row, from the left). Also pictured, seated in the centre, is Lieutenant Commander Eugene Esmonde, VC, DSO, killed in action on 12 February 1942 while leading his bomber squadron against the German fleet escaping Brest in the "Channel Dash."

convoys were, inevitably, crossing the path of the British as they negotiated the waters between Italy and Libya. The Italians had learned from bitter experience to protect their resupply vessels from Fleet Air Arm attacks with extra gunships, making bombing runs increasingly more treacherous for the Fleet Air Arm. The enemy had also started to ramp up the number of air raids on Malta in response to the success of earlier Swordfish attacks.

Being a member of the newly formed 830 Squadron meant taking advantage of the enemy in open water by flying at night, withstanding heavy offensive fire and being somewhat unorthodox in the preparation and execution of operations. That took a certain sort of courage and creativity, not to mention bloody-mindedness. This sat well with the determined and valiant people of Malta. As Bragadin wrote in his history of the Italian Navy in World War II, "Malta proved to be without doubt the principal factor in the Allied victory in the Mediterranean—on land, at sea, and in the air."

The nine men who flew that mission were drawn from all over the UK, most of them being only twenty-one years of age on the night in question. They had little in common except their instructions and their determination to come home.

But sometimes, determination isn't quite enough.

3
FLYING ON EMPTY

"DAMN THIS WEATHER," Wigram muttered, more to himself than to his TAG.

"I don't know that I like this," Griffiths said, "we're going to miss breakfast, aren't we?"

"I rather suspect we are." Wigram tapped the fuel gauge in the hope that it was stuck. They'd been in the air for over five hours and even the familiarity of the Swordfish in his hands wasn't as comforting as usual. A mixture of experience and gut instinct was telling him that they were in more of a bind than he wanted to admit. Putting aside his sense of foreboding and the nagging thought of how quickly they would disappear into the oily, blackness of the sea once their tanks were empty, he piped up with false cheeriness. "Anyway, how are you doing back there?"

"Dreaming of hot, buttered toast and a steaming mug of tea," Griffiths said. "Oh, and I'd quite like it if I was sitting in a patch of sunshine, looking out over Gwrych Castle, after a night canoodling with the prettiest girl in Abergele."

"You're too young to be a hopeless romantic," Wigram laughed. "Leave that for us old boys."

"You may have more hours in the sky than all of us put together," Griffiths told him. "But you still have dreams, don't you?"

"Of course," Wigram replied. "I'm dreaming of terra firma and a runway…"

Anti-aircraft fire strafed the sky beneath them and Osborn's Swordfish moved deftly away from the incoming shells. Wigram followed suit, turning his aircraft away from shore and back out to sea.

"I reckon that was more luck than judgement, wasn't it?" said Griffiths. "It's darker than a coalmine at midnight out there."

"They're probably jumping at shadows," Wigram lied. The waning moon still offered enough light for an eagle-eyed spotter to catch a glimpse of the Stringbags

---

OPPOSITE: Fairey Swordfish flying in formation, No. 1 Naval Air Gunnery School. (LAC)

and that was sufficient to release a barrage of hell their way. "We're too high for them to be a worry to us."

"What does worry you?" Griffiths said unexpectedly.

Wigram took a moment before replying to the young man who always seemed so grown up amongst the hurly-burly of their lives. "Not much, not up here, above it all," Wigram said, gesturing to the expanse ahead of them. "I only worry when I'm home with my good lady and the boys. What kind of future will they have if we don't win this bloody war?"

"Glad I haven't got any nippers yet," said Griffiths. "I wouldn't want to be leaving them behind. I miss all my family back home, like, even though it's a bit noisy and all. Worst thing I had to worry about growing up was whether there'd be holes in the hand-me-downs."

The Stringbag shivered momentarily, passing through a dense cloud bank. Wigram blinked away images of his family, his parents, and his own childhood in Pakistan and India.

"Enough of this maudlin malarky," Wigram said. "Looks like we've got a job to do. Osborn's forming up,"

"It's Clog's turn to make a brew," Griffiths said, his tone relaxed again. "And he does have the gift when it comes to making a perfect cuppa. It must be the Welsh in him. We're all born with good looks and excellent tea-making skills, you know."

"I'm not sure the good folk of Sicily will be rushing to offer us breakfast," Wigram said, manoeuvring into position to make his descent.

"They haven't met us yet. Won't take long before they're serving us polite young chaps fresh bread with lashings of salty butter." Griffiths licked his lips as the aircraft roared low over the waves. "Maybe they'll even have a little honey to spare."

4
AN AVERAGE PILOT

THE SECOND WORLD WAR was heading into a third year and 830 Squadron were deep into their mission to destroy a convoy of merchant ships from the Axis powers: Germany, Italy, and Japan. Success would disrupt the German supply line through the Strait of Sicily, hampering the resupply of their forces in North Africa and reminding everyone that any ship in open water was vulnerable to the tenacity and sheer cussedness of the Royal Navy aircrews.

830 Squadron became particularly good at harrying enemy forces in open waters. As Poolman notes in Night Strike from Malta:

"In September 1941 the Axis had lost twenty-eight percent of all cargoes shipped to Libya, and 830 Squadron had been responsible for a good proportion of that."

By the end of the war, Swordfish were responsible for the destruction of more shipping tonnage than any other aircraft. This was quite the feat for an ageing and obsolete biplane. The efforts of 830 Squadron out of Malta put the Axis supply routes under severe operational stress, leading to a direct impact on the Allied fortunes in North Africa: when the reserves of fuel, ammunition, tanks, and aircraft were low, so were the enemy.

This didn't mean the Swordfish were invincible. Of the seven Swordfish that took off for that mission, three turned back with reported engine problems. With the limited resources available, it was often just a challenge to get the aircraft up and flying.

Of the four aircraft that continued on, Swordfish K8405 was piloted by "Clog" Taylor, just twenty-three years old. In fact, it was his birthday. Born on Armistice Day 1918 in Newport, Wales, he'd been described as "an average pilot" in his logbook. That wasn't a bad thing. It meant he'd passed all the assessments, put in the required number of flying hours, and had shown he could take a plane up and back down again in one piece. It wasn't exactly the rigorous military training military pilots receive today, but enough for him to successfully fly mission after mission. His logbook shows that by 11 November, 1941 he had a total of 497 flying hours, including the seven that he flew that night.

His logbook also showed that his previous flights hadn't been without mishap. In January 1940, there's an entry reporting that he practiced a forced landing in a Tiger Moth. It was all good training for March 1941 when his logbook shows he'd "gone over the side" of the aircraft carrier HMS Furious, crashing his Swordfish into the sea. It seems he misjudged the speed of landing and ending up dropping over the portside edge.

Taylor's Observer, Frank Robinson, had been born in Wandsworth, London, on 19 September 1920. At twenty-one years old, he had already seen a lot of hours in the air. On 23 May that year, he'd flown as Observer with Sub-Lieutenant R G (Bobby) Lawson during the first attack against the infamous unsinkable Bismarck. The records show they'd successfully hit the port quarter as part of the first wave of Swordfish attacks that "softened up" the target.

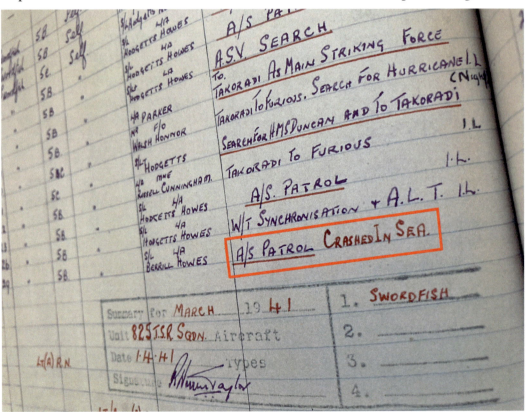

ABOVE: Sub-Lieutenant Taylor's logbook remark – A/S Patrol Crashed in Sea – May 1941.

ABOVE: *The Bismarck, photographed in 1940. (Bundesarchiv)*

Robinson's role in ending the Bismarck's efforts to block Allied supply lines as part of Operation Rheinübung is described in Lawson's obituary in The Scotsman:

Bobby [Lawson], by this time a pilot in the Fleet Air Arm, was one of the avenging forces sent to attack the German ship later that night. In his Swordfish V4295, he was part of the formation of nine aircraft from 825 Squadron that left the new fleet carrier Victorious to carry out their mission (...) When Bobby emerged, his aircraft was alone in the skies but below him the Bismarck was perfectly positioned for him to launch an attack. The German battleship had turned to avoid earlier torpedoes, allowing Bobby to approach from starboard and let loose his torpedo in a single act of determination. His observer, acting Sub Lieutenant F.L. Robinson, witnessed a column of water rise from the Bismarck's starboard side and forever maintained that his torpedo had hit the target.

This obituary corroborates Kennedy's account in his book, *Pursuit: The Sinking of the Bismarck*, where he describes how one of the shadowing Fulmar monoplanes, which had left HMS Victorious after the Swordfish, observed a huge column of water shoot up amidships on Bismarck's starboard side, followed by a burst of black smoke from the funnel. V4295, with the aircraft marking "5L" painted on the side of its fuselage and under the wings, and with Robinson on board, had been one of the first aircraft to attack the 'Giant of the Sea' in advance of its ultimate sinking. But, of course, an attack as audacious as this brought its own challenges. With no way of communicating with HMS Victorious, Lawson and Robinson were unaware that the aircraft carrier had been forced to change direction. When they did finally find it, the engine of the Swordfish cut out as the wheels touched the deck, its fuel tanks empty. This near accident foreshadowed the mission on Armistice Day.

Both Swordfish V4295 and Robinson had proved their worth on that mission before they found themselves in the waters off Cefalù and facing another tricky landing. The frequency with which the men and the aircraft appear in reports indicates the tempo of the conflict and the high rotation of personnel and equipment.

This time, piloting Swordfish V4295 was "Woozle" Osborn who was born on 15 December 1914 in St. Ann's, Lancashire. He showed incredible leadership that night. Although they were lost, with no radio contact and running out of fuel, he kept calm and led the other three pilots towards land whilst thinking about how to keep a little secret away from the enemy: the new "Air to Surface Vessel" (ASV Mk II) detection radar system they were carrying. This system, although discovered by accident in 1937 as part of air-to-air radar testing, was rapidly becoming a critical part of the offensive against Axis shipping vessels. It was an aircraft-mounted radar system used to scan the surface of the ocean to locate ships and surfaced submarines. By 1941, it was being rolled out across the Swordfish squadrons. It was causing havoc for U-boats and played a critical role in locating the Bismarck in the middle of the Atlantic, yet it was still a secret. Osborn made critical decisions that night to protect both the crews and this sensitive piece of equipment.

John Hunt was also with him that night. Born on 18 April 1906 in Hawkhurst, Kent, he was the oldest man on the mission. He was a well-regarded officer who had recently been appointed as Commanding Officer for 830 Squadron, arriving from his role as Chief Instructor on the Observers' course in Arbroath. Although he did not have the same battle experience as Osborn and was unlikely to have received ASV training before he left Arbroath, he was flying as Observer/Navigator for Osborn. This seems odd as his lack of training would have put them all in a difficult position operationally, but we have no way of knowing why this decision was taken. It may simply have been a lack of personnel or resources following the squadron's recent losses. Or it may have been a tactical decision to try out the ASV radar and new R/T between aircraft. None of this operational detail is recorded or available to us.

There was a third man in Swordfish V4295 that night, Matthew Parke an RAF Radar Operator who was flying as the ASV, Wireless Operator that night. Originally from Ballymagroarty, County Londonderry in Northern Ireland, Parke was twenty-one-years-old and a risk-taker, exactly the sort of man needed in a combat situation.

Stewart Campbell, born on 19 May 1921 in Southend-on-Sea in Essex, was the pilot of Swordfish V4421 and something of a determined character. His TAG was Johnny Fallon, another big personality with an infectious grin. A twenty-one-year-old northerner from Ashton-on-Makerfield in Lancashire, he kept a journal during the war which provides us with key first-hand reflections on their lives and actions. He describes how the crew were stationed in Malta and, even though they were on leave, they hadn't had much time for rest before the mission:

> We were on leave in Valletta and we had only just breakfasted when we received a message to return to base at Halfar [Malta]. We bought Armistice Day poppies before boarding the bus...

The fourth aircraft was Swordfish K5979. It was piloted by Aidan Wigram, who was already a commercial pilot before the war so possessed much needed skills and expertise. Aged thirty-four years old, Wigram was the oldest and most experienced crew member after Hunt. His TAG that night was Ken Griffiths, who was twenty-one-years-old and born in Salford, though his family were originally from Wales. Griffiths had eight siblings, and we know that one of his brothers, Gwilym, was also serving.

War makes no consideration for upbringing. These men, from different backgrounds and all corners of Great Britain, found themselves as close-quarters comrades. Brought together for operational reasons and wholly dependent on each other every time they left the relative safety of their station in Malta.

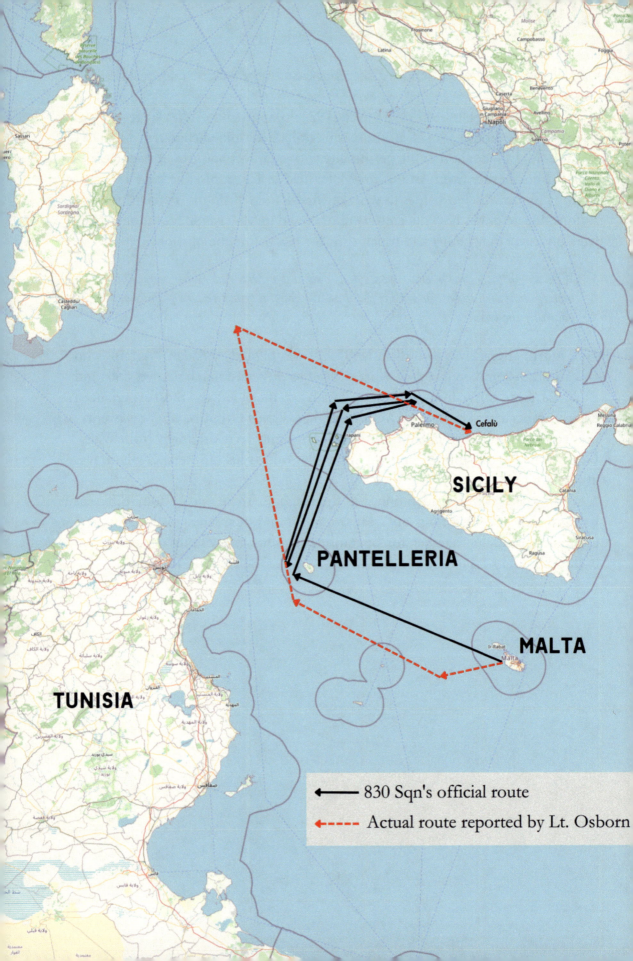

SICILY

PANTELLERIA

MALTA

TUNISIA

Cefalù

←——— 830 Sqn's official route

←- - -- Actual route reported by Lt. Osborn

5
TARGET LOST

"STILL NOTHING?" Osborn called back to Parke.

"Dead space," Parke said, his voice sharp in Osborn's ears.

"Try again and keep trying," Hunt said from his seat at the back of the plane. They looked like a coxless rowing team, lined up in the narrow fuselage, focussed on making it to the finish line.

Parke repeated his transmission over and over, waiting impatiently for some acknowledgement of their morse code finding its mark with Hal Far.

"Are you sure about this course, sir?" Osborn checked with Hunt, knowing this would rile his commanding officer but, with the target lost, and their position uncertain, being barked at was nothing to worry about.

"Yes," said Hunt. "I'm sure! Wind direction has changed. Fly north-west heading three-two-zero degrees. I'm compensating for the drift to get us on Lampedusa."

"Siroccos don't cause a 180 change," Osborn said. "We wouldn't have been flipped around in the opposite direction. Dropped down, drifted sideways, maybe, but not right around." Experience and instinct told him this was the wrong decision. Discipline told him not to countermand an instruction. It didn't mean he was happy about it.

"Make the course correction, Lieutenant Osborn," Hunt instructed. "Now."

The cockpit fell silent as Osborn adjusted course, the three other Swordfish falling in with him to reform a "Finger Four" formation in the black of the night. Osborn could feel the anxiety gnawing at his stomach, one he'd never felt before. But he wasn't going to challenge his commanding officer outright, at least not until he was sure he was right.

They flew on for another hour, talk kept to nothing more than abrupt exchanges between the men.

OPPOSITE: Official and actual route flown by the four Swordfish planes (Marcon, 1998).

"I don't understand how intel could have made this error," Hunt said. "The convoy should have been off Pantelleria."

"And we should have been directly over them," said Osborn.

"I would've expected the ASV to have picked them up, you know," Parke said. "It's a natty piece of equipment."

"Just keep trying the radio," Hunt told him.

"I am," said Parke. "Still no response."

"How many times was this bloody radio tested?" Hunt snapped. He was not his usual, calm self. Osborn had seen him check the coordinates, check his equipment, check the flight plan. He had done everything by the book, but his usual approach hadn't worked and he seemed out of sorts. There had been a strong sirocco wind gusting at over 30 knots on take-off but that hadn't bothered Osborn. The old Stringbag had seen worse. So had Osborn. It was Hunt's job to adjust for the buffeting and turbulence, something he'd done before. Yet still, they were lost and, with three crew onboard, they'd be the first Stringbag to run out of fuel because Hunt was sitting in the seat where the additional fuel tank would have been housed.

"Not tested enough times for us, it seems, but plenty for the men who matter," Parke quipped, trying to lift the mood in the cockpit. "But it wouldn't be much of jolly out if we didn't have something go wrong, now would it?"

"Nat Gold told our Ken about the frequency problems. He tested them and they weren't good," Osborn told them. "Said that when they got east of Malta the signals were weak and then vanished."

"It doesn't matter what Gold thought. We're up here now," said Hunt. "There should be land coming up under us soon."

"Find me a plank of wood and I'll put her down without ruffling your hair, old chap," Osborn said, trying to re-establish some calm in the aircraft. "These beauties are as easy to handle as pushing a pram across the parade ground." He had the confidence of a pilot who had been through some scrapes and the leadership experience of a man who knew that you needed to instil confidence in those around you, even when there was no foundation for it. The basic construction of his aircraft didn't bother him, nor did the lack of comms. In fact, the sheer absurdity of flying so high above the Earth in a contraption made of wire and canvas got his heart racing in the best way.

"There," Hunt shouted, pointing over the side. "There's Lampedusa. We can make a course for Pantelleria now."

Osborn looked down through the clouds and darkness. It was the wrong island. He was sure of it.

"Let's ask Malta for verification," Osborn suggested, trying to keep the sense of frustration out of his voice.

"No," Hunt told him. "No need. I've verified it."

"Parke," Osborn said. "Contact Malta. Confirm position."

"Yes, sir," Parke replied, beginning his morse transmission.

"Look here, Osborn," Hunt shouted. "I don't know what your problem is with taking orders but we have our bearings. Carry out the instruction."

"No reply from Hal Far," Parke told them. "Shall I try again?"

"No need," Osborn said. "We're off route and too far from base to make contact by the seem of things. So, Commander, where do you think we really are?"

The roar of the wind around them rushed in to fill the awkwardness of the pause. Where Hunt should have had a quick and certain response, there was only the drone of the aircraft buffeted by the clouds.

"The Gulf of Sfax," Hunt ventured, more tentative than telling.

Osborn knew that whatever was below them, it wasn't the Gulf of Sfax. He disconnected his Gosport Tube and took the situation in hand, dropping down to 100 feet to confirm for himself that the wind was still blowing a strong south-easterly and that the island at the last known checkpoint, overflown 120 minutes earlier, was Pantelleria. He was right. They had been flying towards Sardinia all this time, not Sicily. With the headwind and the lack of fuel, Malta was no longer an option. He reconnected his Gosport.

"Setting a route east-south-east," he told Hunt. "Heading for Sicily. Looking for a place to land." Hunt did not respond. "Parke, let the others know they'll need to ditch their torpedoes."

"Roger," Parke replied just as anti-aircraft fire lit up the sky around them.

"Heading back out to sea," Osborn told them. "We'll look for somewhere further along the coast." He checked his fuel gauge: it was barely registering.

The edge of Sicily came in and out of view through the clouds. The further they tracked along the coastline, the more likely they were to be hit by gunfire or the aircraft stuttering to a stall as it ran out of fuel. Osborn had one last decision to make.

"Prepare for a forced landing," Osborn instructed Parke, reducing altitude and speed. "I'm ditching at sea. They're not getting their bloody hands on the ASV."

6
DEAD SPACE

FROM THE AIR, THE STRAIT OF SICILY on a sunny day is a ribbon of silver. Stunning scenery laid out in a green-brown patchwork below the fuselage, sunlight dappling along the undulating water, birds drifting lazily on gentle thermals. On the night of 11 November 1941, the weather conditions were poor, the sort that would make any pilot think twice about leaving the ground. Any aircraft taking off would face unpredictable wind, cloudy sky, and the likelihood of the weather worsening the further you are from the airfield. For the Swordfish crews, the weather was just as much of a threat as the enemy.

Unexpected gusting winds from the south pushed the Swordfish off-track and were the catalyst for the formation of four remaining Swordfish to become temporarily unsure of their position. Their drift off course was then exacerbated by Hunt's navigational error, resulting in an inability to locate their targets. Yet, Hunt was clearly an excellent navigator. Leading Airman Nat Gold, the TAG in one of the Swordfish that returned early that night, stated in his memoirs that it was Hunt's navigational skills on the mission that enabled him to return safely to Malta due to some "engine troubles" (this was Gold's euphemism for the decision of the pilot "who shall not be named" flying their Swordfish and who was known to turn back even when he didn't need to). As Gold says:

> [Lieutenant-Commander] Hunt saved our lives, the course he gave was unbelievably spot on, it could not have been more perfect.

Although Hunt's reported navigational skills and service record indicate he was more than capable of leading the mission, it seems that Osborn and Hunt did not see eye to eye. Fallon reported in his own memoirs that they were distant

---

OPPOSITE: Layer of charged electrons (Ionosphere) which permit High-Frequency skywave propagation (MIT, 2018).

with each other on that mission. This is confirmed in Spooner's book, *Faith, Hope and Malta*, which describes an almost mutinous atmosphere and Osborn taking command decisions without Hunt. Spooner was the pilot of the Wellington that was sent up from Malta with the seven Swordfish at the start of the mission to act as spotter. He made it back in one piece along with the three other Swordfish crews who returned due to technical problems.

But the weather was only one of the external factors that came together to bring the aircraft to the shores of Cefalù.

The on-board HF radio also let them down. Badly. During test flights it had been reported as having dead spots. These reports were ignored, much to the consternation of the pilots. Nat Gold wrote in his memoir:

> *Sometime previously, I and an Observer had been asked to test a new frequency, I to fly in one Swordfish and the Observer in another…We took off during darkness and flew in the vicinity of Grand Harbour, the reception was good, R5, too good I thought, after a while we received a coded signal to take up a position East of Malta due to an imminent air raid. …the Observer constantly sent messages, but some were weak from this short distance out from land, a gut feeling kept telling me something was not quite right about this frequency, but I couldn't pinpoint it. When we eventually landed and reported to the Senior Observer, I expressed my feelings of doubt, as we were sitting on top of the transmitter it would have been more beneficial if we had travelled further away. The Observer considered it to be an excellent frequency and I got the impression that rank prevailed.*

> *Eventually we changed to this new frequency with frightening results, we nearly lost several aircraft in one go, some landed with only a teaspoonful of petrol left in their tanks, they all had great difficulty in communicating with Malta. It transpired that this frequency had what is called a "Dead Space" over Malta. When the morse key is pressed to make contact a radio wave is emitted from the aerial in what is known as a C.W. (continuous wave). These waves leave the earth at a regular angle travelling upwards in the atmosphere and are reflected downwards from the ionosphere at a similar regular angle; where there is a dead space, the wave bounces back from the ionosphere at an acute angle. This is what was happening over Malta and both aircraft and ground station were having great difficulty communicating with one another.*

Compared to the pilots today, who only use HF frequencies when outside VHF range and with a backup frequency available, the Swordfish crews had no chance of contacting Hal Far base in Malta. The difficulties they faced, like so many aviation disasters, inform operations today. This can be seen in the following extracts from the current HF Management Guidance Material manual.

2.3.4.1 Aircraft stations shall operate on the appropriate radio frequencies.

1.8 Sky wave propagation in the HF band (3 to 30 MHz) is complicated…

1.8.4 For good long-range HF R/T reception a frequency must be chosen which will not suffer too much attenuation…

1.8.5 … a frequency is chosen which is as high as possible without exceeding the MUF (Maximum Usable Frequency) for the path between the transmitter and distant receiver. The MUF is that frequency, for the prevailing conditions, which produces a skip zone (the "Dead Space" referred to previously in TAG N Gold's memoir) extending just short of the distant receiver. Any higher frequency would give a higher critical angle and a greater skip distance exceeding beyond the receiver, which would then lose that sky wave contact with the transmitter.

1.8.6 MUF at night is much less than by day…

1.9 The theoretical range for HF frequencies varies, depending on the propagation path used, ground or sky waves, Ground waves usually can reach up to 100 nautical miles (nm) and sky waves longer distances, however, sky waves will not be received within the skip distance (probably several hundred miles from the transmitter). The theoretical

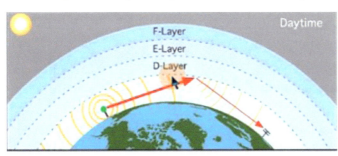

maximum range obtained by means of a single reflection from the E layer is about 1,300 nm, and from the F layer about 2,500 nm.

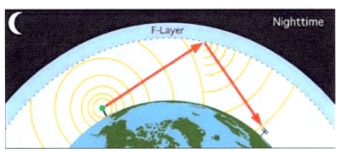

ABOVE: A different HF frequency must be used at night to reach the same receiver (OfficialSWLchannel, 2017).

With their developing knowledge of HF signals and lack of time to test equipment in live situations, it was no surprise that mistakes were made. In his memoir, Fallon states that he thought they were too far from Malta for their signal

ABOVE: Presumed Skip Zone and confirmed range achieved with the wrong HF frequency used by 830 Squadron (L Lazzara, 2023).

to be heard. Ironically, the HF frequency they were using was for long-range communication, so they were actually too close for it to be effective. But their signals were not lost – they were picked up by Gibraltar and Alexandria! Neither station was much help at such distances.

Blown off-course, failing to locate the target and without radio contact, the men of the Swordfish mission were flying blind. They stayed in formation, keeping each other company while their fuel gauges dropped, and their chances of detection rose. If they weren't spotted and shot out of the sky, they'd most likely drop into the sea with no one ever knowing what happened to them.

In Spooner's book he provides confirmation that Osborn's aircraft, V4295, was the only one fitted with ASV radar and was not carrying a torpedo. Both of these are unusual details. Leaving base without a torpedo would indicate that the primary objective of V4295 was not to lay down munitions or that there was a shortage of torpedoes. Also, very few aircraft had the ASV radar at the time or the experimental radio telephony (R/T) radio between

ABOVE: Leading Airman Nat Gold, seen at Hal Far, Malta.

26

aircraft. Osborn would have been keen to keep all of this intelligence away from the enemy. Nat Gold also gives a detail in his memoir that helps explain some of the choices that night:

"Seven Swordfish left Malta, led by Lieutenant/Cmdr. Hunt. For the very first time we were using R/T between aircraft."

It would have been quite something if this intelligence had fallen into the hands of the enemy. The ability to use R/T for voice communication between planes in flight, using airwaves rather than cables (somewhat of a challenge in flight!), together with the ASV radar would have allowed for much more co-ordinated attack strategies. The advantages of this would have been more accurate detection of smaller vessels at sea plus more successful strike rates, reducing

Lt. George Myles Thomas "Woozle" Osborn

wasted munitions and fuel use. All of these would provide both marginal and maximal gains at the mid-point of the war, something Rommel could not allow.

Hunt's skills had already saved the lives of Nat Gold and the "pilot who shall not be named" that night with his accurate guidance. But after this, something had gone seriously awry with his calculations and his instructions that had flown them towards Sardinia rather than Sicily. Such an error is at odds with his previous combat performance. Exactly a month earlier he'd led a highly successful mission that led to the sinking of the Italian steamships Zena and Casaregis. Despite his lack of combat experience, he clearly had the ability to lead and to execute the mission, but maybe a touch of obstinance while flying blind in the night sky and without HF radio meant he could not see his navigational error in time to correct it. Or maybe it was just that on that night, skills and bravery alone were not enough.

Whatever the cause of the problem, Osborn was left to make the final command decision. They would deliberately ditch their Stringbag at sea.

7
FINDING CEFALÙ

"WE'RE GOING TO NEED TO DROP THE TORPEDO," Campbell told Fallon. "Parke's signalled – abort and look for land and wherever we end up, we won't want that under us."

"Roger, that," Fallon replied. He'd been hanging over the side of the aircraft again, still trying to spot the target but to no avail. They were now so far off track that it was more important to find a way down and fight another day than to chase a target that had eluded them all night. 830 Squadron had lost too many planes and men of late. Far too many.

"Signal Hal Far. Let them know we're ditching it," Campbell said, "I think we're coming up on Palermo but...I really don't know" He'd been following Osborn even though it was beginning to feel like they were on a joyride up and down the Italian islands.

"We're still transmitting blind," Fallon told him as he tapped out the repeated message in morse code.

"Understood," Campbell replied. "Osborn is taking us east. He must have something in mind because we're not going to make it back to Malta in this headwind."

"Roger," Fallon said, signalling to the other crews that they were dropping their "tin fish." The torpedo fell away into the darkness beneath them, the aircraft lifting slightly as the load lessened. The weight of their unfinished mission released, they flew in silence, letting the night slide over them, the clouds and wind jostling them like wooden toys in a tin bath. Fallon in his battledress and Campbell in his flying jacket, their uniforms offering little warmth or protection against the elements or the enemy.

"What's your favourite song?" Campbell asked Fallon, gently correcting the path of the Swordfish to sit further back in the formation, as though he was

OPPOSITE: Cefalù lighthouse. (C. Cucci, 2014)

moving a piece on a chess board in a game that had gone on for too long.

"For singing or dancing?" Fallon sang out in a vaguely operatic voice. His ability to start a party in the bar or on a street corner was the stuff of many a good-hearted anecdote, his smile the start of many a lively and entertaining evening.

"Singing," said Campbell. "We're not going to be dancing in here. Not enough room to swing a cat let alone a girl, is there?" He rapped on the fuselage with his gloved knuckles and then started tracing the snug cockpit with his hand, like he was remembering something.

"You old curmudgeon. A good dance would warm us up," Fallon called back. "Mind you, it wouldn't be much fun doing the Lindy Hop without a girl to keep me company."

"Come on, what's your favourite song, Johnny?" Campbell scanned around him to make sure the other three planes were where he expected them to be. They'd already had too many moments when the weather had pulled them apart with an unexpected air pocket or cloud bank. Losing contact now would be the tin hat on the whole thing.

"You are my sunshine," Fallon sang out again, this time in a tremulous baritone. "The wonderful Gene Autry, no less."

"Splendid choice. Start singing. And give it some gusto," Campbell told him. "Why?"

"Because wherever we land, we're going to make an entrance so we might as well put on a show," Campbell said. "Hello, looks like this it. We're going in."

A light flashed out from Osborn's aircraft.

"A show, you say?" Fallon declared in theatrical style. "We can do that. You fly, I'll sing. Everyone will know we're coming in…"

You are my sunshine, my only sunshine,
You make me happy when skies are grey,
You'll never know dear how much I love you,
Please don't take my sunshine away…

OPPOSITE: Sub-Lieutenant Stewart Campbell. (Campbell Family)

82·IDRO·186·AUGUSTA·24·IV·930·ORE 16· CEFALÙ

8
AMEN

"TRY THE RADIO AGAIN," Wigram told Griffiths,

"Wilco." Griffiths repeated the message that he'd already been sending. He hadn't stopped trying all night and Griffiths hadn't stopped telling him to try. It wasn't that Wigram doubted Griffiths, more that he liked to check things for himself. "Amen," Griffiths said solemnly as he finished transmitting.

"Amen indeed. Now prepare for a bumpy ride in," Wigram said, scanning the seemingly placid sea beneath them. There were no clues, nothing to navigate off. The distance from the wheels to the surface was impossible to gauge and there was no way of knowing if any rocks or vessels were in their way. There could be waves, rip tides, submerged rocks, or enemy vessels anywhere in the area, but from where he was sitting, it looked strangely like he was heading for an endless lake of black cake icing. Not that they were unprepared for such eventualities. It wasn't his first forced landing and he doubted it would be his last.

The water rose up towards them, faster than he'd been expecting and he adjusted his speed and angle of descent. The aircraft shuddered momentarily, groaned and seemed to take control, his hands no longer making the decisions.

"You might want to say another prayer," Wigram shouted. "I am."

OPPOSITE: Aerial photograph of Cefalù taken in 1930 by Salvatore Barracato, a Second World War photographer for the Regia Aeronautica (Barracato Family).

9
FISHING FOR PILOTS

"IF I'M NOT MISTAKEN," Parke said, shifting cautiously in the dinghy, "that's Italian." He rubbed at his shoulder that had taken a bit of a battering as they'd hit the water.

"Siete piloti? Siete Inglesi?"

"It seems we didn't make it to Malta after all," Osborn said to Hunt, sarcasm edging his voice as they all strained to hear the voices coming ever closer.

"Mani in alto! Mani in alto!"

"That's definitely Italian," Parke said, "and they sound pretty excited about something."

"Us," Hunt snarled, one hand on his pistol and the other clutching an oar. "We've dropped out of the sky and we're floating around in a dinghy disturbing their fish. They're just fishermen. We'd have been shot by now if they were soldiers."

"I can't see any of the other chaps, or planes," Osborn said, shading his eyes against the early morning sun breaking through the pillows of cloud above them. "You're right, they're just fishermen. Looks like three of them on board."

"I bet they've got good coffee and some of that splendid fresh Italian bread," Parke mused, watching the approaching boat as his stomach rumbled.

"And they might have weapons under their lobster pots," Hunt said, reaching for his revolver. "Look alive, we don't know how this will go."

***

It went well.

The only thing the fisherman wanted that day from Osborn, Hunt and Parke were their parachute silks, to make shirts. Everything is useful in a war.

Especially intelligence.

OPPOSITE: Overflying Cefalù en-route to Malta with Mount Etna in the background. (Lazzara, 2022)

Ditching at sea ensured that the ASV radar, maps and the Stringbag could not be examined by the enemy. Osborn was already showing his colours as a man with a keen understanding of what was valuable in a conflict. He was also demonstrating his willingness to act independently by challenging authority and being single-minded in his execution of a task. He had been ready to go up against Hunt even if it set them against each other.

Osborn had also been ready for a fist fight, planning to overpower the fisherman and make their escape. But a night of high adrenaline flying and an unfortunate ditching into the Mediterranean had left him exhausted and unable to use his legs. Making an escape would have to wait.

Bedraggled and with no way of striking out for home, the three men found themselves the biggest catch the fishermen had ever landed. The tense boat ride to shore was brief, giving them little chance to become acquainted with their affable captors. Reaching the beach, they could see there was a welcoming committee of soldiers. Their war was about to change completely.

OPPOSITE: How pilots today would fly the route flown by 830 Squadron, using GPS waypoints (e.g., MEGAN, GIANO) and airways (e.g., M735). (Luca Lazzara)

10
Sicilian Charm

"IT'S GOING TO BE A WET ONE, JOHNNY!" shouted Campbell, as he guided the Stringbag towards the glassy surface of the sea.

"Keep us off the bottom and I'll polish your boots for a month," Fallon shouted back, the sputtering of the stalling engine vibrating through his ribcage as he braced himself for impact.

"That's the plan," said Campbell, sitting square in his seat, trying not to strain forward no matter how much his instinct made him tense up. He kept replaying all the practice runs for water landings, the drills, the SOPs. Relax into it, his instructor had said. You'll float down like a feather on the breeze if you just relax. That's what the grumpy, old instructor with the broken nose had told him. What he'd failed to tell him was that his heart would be hammering its way out of his chest and his stomach would be flipping like a pancake.

"Feeling splendid back here," Fallon called out, not a trace of fear or anxiety in his tone. It was like he was on the charabanc for a bit of Sunday sightseeing. Campbell had always admired that quality in him: the ability to fit right in, whatever the situation.

"Approach is good," Campbell said. "Airspeed is…" He was cut off by a flash of light to their starboard side. "What was that?"

"No idea," Fallon said. "Can't tell if it was us or them."

"We're coming in," Campbell called out, taking deliberate breaths to focus himself. "Make ready for a speedy exit as soon as we're down."

"Roger that, old chap," Fallon said. "More than happy to oblige."

"Nearly there. Nearly there. Nearly there…"

***

OPPOSITE: Photograph taken on 12 November, 1941, showing the Cefalù railway line, above the beach. Fairey Swordfish K8405, upside down on the beach, can be seen in the middle distance.

Cefalù is beautiful. A typical Sicilian coastal town with the blue sea lapping the beach, red-tiled roofs topping the houses nestled against each other, a cathedral and a lighthouse, generous piazzas, and generous people. It's a lovely holiday destination today that encourages British visitors.

For the men of 830 Squadron, it was cold, hostile, and deadly.

Four Swordfish roaring towards the coast would have been unexpected and unwelcome. Although the Italian soldiers stationed there would have known there was a possibility of enemy aircraft, they would also have known that the small civilian population was of little strategic interest to Allied forces. When the aircraft flew out of the clouds, low, in trouble, and possibly carrying unexploded ordnance, the local military would have been few and far between, with their fingers very much on the triggers.

Campbell and Fallon made it down.

Having firmly ditched the aircraft on an even keel, the two men were able to scramble out of the plane onto the wing only to be greeted by gunfire. With the Swordfish intact but sinking, they climbed aboard their dinghy which had inflated on impact. More gunfire punctured the air around them, so they kept low, still and silent.

But it was already too late for any attempt at stealth. Their dinghy, struck by one of the bullets, was deflating rapidly and the Stringbag was going down in a rush of briny bubbles. Still uninjured, but now with no useful method of transportation left, they had little choice but to swim for shore and whatever reception awaited them. The Mediterranean Sea had the bite of winter and they had to kick off their heavy boots to swim away from their rapidly vanishing aircraft, hoping that there were no enemy boats between them and land.

Readying themselves for an unfriendly welcome, after a hard swim they hauled themselves onto the beach and surveyed the immediate area. It was deserted. For all the angry shooting, there were no soldiers guarding the rocky shoreline where they had crawled out. They paused long enough to check for the other crews but couldn't see them or the other aircraft. Heading for the cliffs, they climbed up in heart-stopping haste, soaking wet, with no boots on their feet and no idea where they were going. At the top, they took cover in a stubby hedgerow, sleeping in turns until it was light. It lacked the charm of a seaside boarding house in Margate but it was safer than their other options. Setting off come morning, they almost immediately stumbled across a set of tracks with a train heading for them. They dove for cover in some sparse shrubs and watched the slow-moving train, filled with troops, going west. Giving themselves a few moments to regain their composure, they started walking again, now hyper-vigilant for the enemy. They followed a narrow track heading east, skirting around a towering rock face and coming face-to-face with a large number of troops forming up into search parties. As Fallon says in the memoir he left for his son:

> *They must have been as surprised as we were! Having been seen by scores of eyes, with no possibility of escape, we could only surrender. There was no force used, everything was quite civilized. We were searched and then escorted along the railway line for about a mile to a little telephone exchange.*

As they walked, local people came to their doors to watch the captives being marched into town. Some of the women were crying, which unnerved Campbell, even though they knew that two of their squadron had been taken prisoner in Sicily a month earlier. Fallon hoped that it was just that the sight of two bedraggled airmen, their wet uniforms stained blood-red from the fluorescent sea markers sewn into their Mae Wests, was enough to upset the quiet folk of the coastal town.

At the telephone exchange, some more locals joined them, trying to strike up an inquisitive conversation, but their escorts shooed them away. They were a novelty and clearly not dangerous in their bedraggled state but, still, they were the enemy.

When the Carabinieri arrived to take them to the police station, the serious business of interrogation started. It lasted for several hours but Fallon does not report how it was conducted. They were then passed on to the Italian Air Force who escorted them to their new quarters in the Grand Hotel in Palermo. They had separate bedrooms with a connecting bathroom, manned by a guard at all times. Their captives were generous and civilised, providing shaving gear, clean sheets, good food and a pair of boots for each of them to replace the ones they'd kicked off as they swam ashore. Fallon was quite taken by the big bath towels and the juicy, sweet oranges in the nearby trees. In the morning, they were allowed into the garden to kick a football around and at lunchtime they were escorted to a bar and allowed one drink. They were required to sign for these and they chose the names "Joseph Stalin" and "Winston S. Churchill". With their glasses raised they would declare, "Churchill will pay!" to the amusement of the bar staff. Their evenings included a visit from members of the Italian air crews, boasting about their actions over Malta that day. Fallon and Campbell took these claims with "a pinch of salt" and gave a wry smile to each other.

11
LOST

WIGRAM AND GRIFFITHS HIT THE WATER, HARD.

There was little chance of escape as their Swordfish burst into flames and sank. This was long before our era of black boxes, GPS trackers and fire-retardant materials. There would have been no protection against the impact of the crash or the subsequent explosion and the location of the aircraft would have been impossible to pinpoint.

The very nature of the Stringbag, reassuringly basic and reliable, was its greatest shortcoming as it offered minimal protection for the crew, both in flight and in the event of a forced landing. No protective armour, not even a canopy over their heads to keep out the rain. Air crew needed to be physically and mentally tough just to undertake their missions. Attempting a water landing in enemy territory on low fuel and poor visibility would have been a terrifying prospect for any pilot, experienced or not. At thirty-four years of age, with more experience of commercial and military flying than the other men in the squadron, Aidan Wigram died, leaving a wife and two sons behind. The body of the man who had studied at Cambridge and who had been the mentor of the team was never recovered.

Ken Griffiths died with him. Neither was his body ever found. Aircraft crashes were not uncommon, and all crew trained for forced landings and water landings. So, it's no surprise that this wasn't the first Swordfish crash that Griffiths had experienced. He'd been with Commander Charles Lamb, over Egypt in 1940, when disaster had struck. As Lamb wrote in his memoirs *War in the Stringbag*:

> *The last time this had happened had been in the dark, with Ken Griffiths in the back seat too. […] Before landing, I had time to yell at Ken, "You must be a Jonah!".*

OPPOSITE: Lieutenant A.F. Wigram, pictured on his wedding day in 1938.

43

And then again, in January 1941 when Lamb and Griffiths were shot down and ended up ditching, Lamb describes how:

"The Observer and the TAG [Griffiths] were catapulted through the air and splashed into the sea about twenty yards ahead of the Swordfish".

They survived that crash, but only just. After ditching their plane and jumping into the dinghy, they waited for rescue and, as a ship plucked them out of the water, their plane exploded. They had forgotten to drop the depth charge and, as that Swordfish started to sink, the charge detonated. Maybe the same thing happened again on 11 November 1941. Perhaps the aircraft exploded on contact with the sea or hit submerged rocks.

Whatever happened, Aidan Wigram and Ken Griffiths were lost that night. Forever.

OPPOSITE: Leading Airman Ken Griffiths (right).

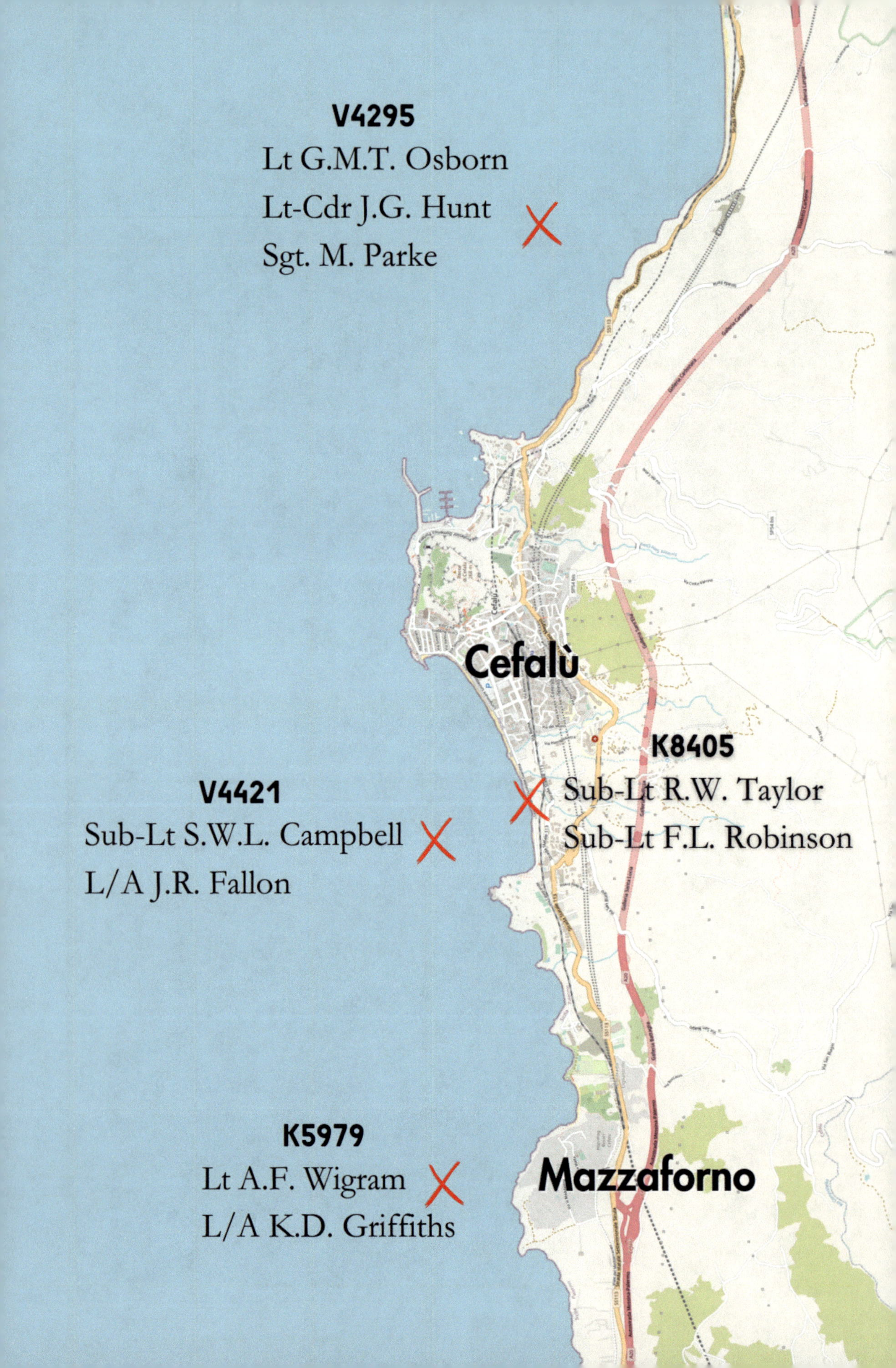

V4295

Lt G.M.T. Osborn

Lt-Cdr J.G. Hunt

Sgt. M. Parke

✗

Cefalù

K8405

Sub-Lt R.W. Taylor

Sub-Lt F.L. Robinson

✗

V4421

Sub-Lt S.W.L. Campbell ✗

L/A J.R. Fallon

K5979

Lt A.F. Wigram ✗

L/A K.D. Griffiths

Mazzaforno

12
MISSING

FOUR AIRCRAFT AND NINE MEN were recorded as missing in the Malta War Diary the next day:

> *Overnight, seven Swordfish from 830 Squadron Fleet Air Arm at Hal Far were despatched to attack a convoy consisting of two merchant vessels west of Pantelleria. Three aircraft returned to base owing to engine trouble; the remaining four failed to return to base. The missing crews are Lieutenant Cmdr Hunt, Lieutenant Osborn, Lieutenant Wigram, S/Lieutenant Campbell, S/Lieutenant Taylor, S/Lieutenant Robinson, Sgt Parke, L A Fallon and L A Griffiths.*
>   *- 12 November 1941 - Air War Losses and Gains reported in Malta War Diary*

The map at left shows the confirmed locations of the aircraft, almost in a line, with Osborn ditching furthest from land. It was a serious blow to the already seriously depleted Swordfish squadron, but it didn't stop the remaining crews from continuing to be a problem to the enemy, flying night after night, almost on a wing and a prayer. As Cameron, in Wings of the Morning, says about the squadron, "…830's handful of Swordfish had acted as a tourniquet on Rommel's supply line." Their tenacity left the Afrika Korps desperate for supplies and prompted Mussolini to ask for help from the Luftwaffe. Worse, Field Marshal Kesselring, on arriving in Sicily in 1941, declared that Malta was to be "Coventrated" – a reference to the decimation of Coventry when it had been reduced to rubble by air bombardment. Thus, the success of 830 Squadron brought its own downside. While the men of the Swordfish who crashed on Armistice night 1941 were becoming accustomed to life as PoWs, Malta was pounded. Mercilessly. In the early months of 1942, there were 107 large-scale air raids over Malta, many lasting for eight hours. The airfield became a series of craters and burnout buildings, but the pilots kept on taking to the skies. Of the serviceable aircraft, the squadron was

OPPOSITE: Map of approximate Swordfish crash locations.

eventually reduced to just one Swordfish—but it kept flying, kept doing damage, and kept the Axis forces on alert.

This increase in attacks on Malta would have been particularly important to Hunt because Malta was where he married Marjorie Naylor Farrant in 1932 at the Holy Trinity Church in Sliema. Although Marjorie and their children had moved to Falmouth at the outbreak of the war, Hunt had good reason to want to get back to defend the island that was his home.

Losing any asset in battle is a problem. Losing so many men and planes in one night was a human and operational tragedy. Not only had the four aircraft and crew crashed, but Gold reports in his memoir that a Wellington bomber and two other aircraft from the squadron had gone missing as well. The targets had not been acquired, the new radio frequency had failed, and Fleet Air Arm had no idea where their crews had ditched.

OPPOSITE: Local fisherman walking close to the damaged engine of Swordfish K8405 with Cefalù's twelfth-century Cathedral in the background.

13
MIXED BLESSINGS

"BUGGER IT," Robinson said, straining to release himself from the safety wire clipped to the harness between his legs. "Bloody jockstrap won't let me go." He was upside down, held precariously by the jockstrap configuration, and in danger of breaking his neck with a hasty exit onto the rocky beach. "Ah, there we go," he said, finally unclipping himself and bracing against the fuselage that had come to rest on solid ground. "Oh, hello, I think we've pranged the old girl."

"Everything okay there, Frank?" Taylor asked, easing himself out of the cockpit and curling down onto the portside wing before scrambling to his feet on the beach. He staggered and clutched at the wheel strut.

"That was one hell of a landing, Clog," said Robinson, following Taylor onto the wing. The sense of being out of kilter took a while to settle as his eyes adjusted to the landscape. He brushed himself down and stepped back to take a better look at the aircraft. The Swordfish was tipped belly up but resting perfectly on the top wing. It was like a giant had flipped them over with a playful hand. The beach around them was a mix of rocks and sand, with the sea a few yards behind the prostrate Swordfish, and the foam of the tide just shy of the nose. He could hear a strange pounding noise, fast and close. He looked around in confusion until he realised it was just the sound of his own blood pumping in his ears.

"Shame about these fellows," Taylor said, slapping a large boulder. "I'd have kept her on her toes if they hadn't been in the way."

"Thanks for keeping us in one piece," Robinson said, extending his hand. Taylor shook it, briefly.

"Don't understand why there wasn't any ack-ack fire as we came in," Taylor said, lifting his eyes to check around them.

"Maybe they're having a night off," Robinson said, his pulse rate dropping

OPPOSITE: Illustration of Sub-Lt Taylor's capture on the beach of Cefalù (Il Mattino Illustrato, December 1941).

and his urge to run receding. "Let me just square away the Bigsworth in case anyone is around." Shots rang out in the distance.

"Make it quick," Taylor said, turning to look behind them, searching beyond the white froth breaking on the dark beach. "We'd better get away from the old girl and find cover. Can you see the others anywhere?"

"I can't see anything," Robinson said, ripping up charts and maps and scattering them into the wind. "I'm pretty sure Campbell was coming in behind us, but I lost sight of Osborn and Wigram."

"There was a flash portside," Taylor said. "But I can't tell you if it was one of us going down or one of them firing up."

"The locals aren't going to be too pleased with us dropping in uninvited," Robinson said. "And we're a bit limited for weapons. The Vickers will be useless, it's underneath the Stringbag, and I don't think we can hold off a troop of irritated Italians with just our revolvers."

"You have a point. Let's find somewhere out of sight while we plan our next move," Taylor said, pulling his flying jacket straight and raking his fingers through his hair.

"Shall we track along the beach or climb up the cliff?" Robinson asked, running his hand over the Swordfish. He knew he wouldn't be seeing her again and that she would soon be stripped down and cannibalised. It wasn't a fitting end for such a loyal aircraft.

"Along the beach and then inland," Taylor said. "We'll stand a better chance of finding cover further down. I just don't understand why they're not all over us already."

A shout went up somewhere ahead of them.

"They will be soon," Robinson said, as they began running.

OPPOSITE: Swordfish K8405 being inspected by Italian forces.

14
THE GAME'S UP

NOT ONLY DID GROUND CREW BACK AT BASE in Malta have no way of knowing what had finally happened to their boys, the crew had no way of knowing if their radio signals had been received, intercepted, or just lost in the atmosphere. They had been transmitting blind, and ultimately landing blind.

Setting down the Swordfish on Sicily was a series of near impossible challenges. No clear indication of where the land began and the sea ended, no idea what sort of ground would meet their wheels, no fuel to circle around for another attempt, possible enemy fire from the ground, and possible buildings and other obstacles in the way of their graceful descent. It was a point and hope situation.

Unless of course, you were an "average pilot" in the Fleet Air Arm.

Taylor landed his Swordfish on the rocky beach of Cefalù, executing a skilled and brilliant touchdown, much more than an average pilot would have mustered. And then he bumped into some unfriendly boulders and his aircraft flipped over, coming to rest upside down, wheels in the air, in an unorthodox but ultimately life-saving piece of piloting.

Taylor and Robinson only had a harness strapping them into their seats. It would have prevented them from catapulting out of the aircraft in the unceremonious encounter with the boulders but would probably have left them bruised, to say the least. The landing on uneven ground and then being tipped upside down would have been bone shaking and disorientating. But they didn't have time to take a breath or tend to any wounds.

Their approach had been spotted by the Italian defending force on Sicily who mobilised immediately to intercept them.

Once they were on land, the game was up for Taylor and Robinson. They were met at gunpoint by Italian soldiers and taken away to be interrogated while their Stringbag became the site of intense interest for both the Italian army and the local people. The photographs from the scene show the aircraft being inspected by

OPPOSITE: Local children playing near Swordfish K8405, 1941.

soldiers while crowds of civilians gather in the background. It caused quite a stir at the time and is still a talking point in the town to this day.

Three Swordfish sank on the mission, and one ended its days in a prone position on the beach of Cefalù. Like the pilots, these planes had seen a lot of action in their short time flying out of Hal Far.

V4295 had been fitted with long range fuel tanks and the ASV radar, as part of 825 Squadron which were the first to be fitted with the ASV, before it flew off from HMS Ark Royal on 25th July 1941 to join the depleted 830 Squadron in Malta. These modifications gave V4295 the operational capability to undertake the mission and made it a high value asset. The decision to ditch was courageous and operationally sound.

The sea, the frenzy of war, and the passage of time meant that the last resting places of the Swordfish went unknown for many years. That was until Professor Gianfranco Purpura of Palermo University made the initial discovery of the wrecks in the late 1960s. Subsequently, the Italian historian, Tullio Marcon, in his article in 1998, established that the Swordfish that had ditched in the Calura area in Cefalù was the one flown by Osborn. This is corroborated by a letter received by Marcon from Osborn on 22nd May 1989. Further confirmation of the registration and crew of V4295 was provided during the writing of this book in an e-mail from retired Lieutenant-Commander M. Tennant, curatorial volunteer of the Fleet Air Arm Museum. The written memoirs and artifacts left by the airmen with their families

ABOVE: Bottom of fuselage, Swordfish V4295 (confirmed by Ray Polidano, Malta Aviation Museum and Prof Purpura, Palermo University)

ABOVE: *Fragment of aircraft recovered from Mazzaforno, in Cefalù. Presumed to be part of the Swordfish flown by Lieutenant Wigram and L/A Griffiths. Fragment recovered by Professor Purpura (other artefacts left in situ).*

confirm that, strategically, Osborn chose to ditch away from the coast to prevent the Italian forces capturing the ASV radar onboard his plane.

As the thin light of morning appeared, the men were operating alone, unsure of where each crew had landed and unable to contact each other. It was only when, three days later, the remaining survivors were brought to the Grand Hotel that they were able to piece together the sequence of events. It wasn't an entirely happy and harmonious reunion. Fallon notes that:

> …*the senior pilot and the C.O. seemed to be very serious and distant with each other, neither of them saying what was wrong. (I learned later that the Senior Pilot had questioned the course he was given by the C.O. and he was told to mind his own business).*

All of the men were then "wined and dined by the Top Brass" at the Regia Aeronautica HQ (Italian Royal Air Force). Shaken by the crash and the stress of running the gauntlet of being captured, the Italian military hospitality must have been most welcome. This moment of calm was fleeting. The next day they were moved out to an interrogation camp near Rome and joined by the sole survivor from a Wellington that had ditched on its way to the Middle East. He was seventeen years old, Jewish, and alone. Fallon took responsibility for him, instructing him to keep on saying, "I am English" for fear of what would happen if their captors discovered he was a Jew. Fallon also describes how they were shown the English newspapers, confirming that the Ark Royal had been sunk by a submarine. The juxtaposition of civility and fear is casual in Fallon's account with no mention of the effect of being interrogated. Even when they were put under pressure by interrogators, Fallon remained measured. He describes questions about:

> ...a Form 700 which had been retrieved from a crashed Blenheim (this document shouldn't have been in the aircraft). There was an entry in it saying "I.F.F. fitted", and the Italians wanted to know what it meant. I had to constantly plead ignorance, knowing full-well what it meant.

An IFF was the Identification Friend or Foe system. The FuG 25a Esrtlin IFF was originally developed by German scientists for the Luftwaffe. It's something of a misnomer as, initially, it could only positively identify friendly forces. If there was battle damage, equipment failure or interference with the signal, the IFF could not guarantee a correct identification. Unfortunately for the Germans, British military scientists improved on the technology very quickly using coded radar signals (called Cross-Band Interrogation, or CBI) to automatically trigger a response from any FuG 25a systems in the vicinity. It then used the response signal to determine the aircraft's direction and range. Add to this the new generation ASV (Air-to-Surface-Vessel) radar that the Swordfish was carrying, capable of detecting much smaller objects than earlier versions, and Fallon did well to plead ignorance. This type of intelligence would have given the Italians crucial information about the capacity of British detection equipment.

It's hard to say why Osborn decided to head for Cefalù, taking the whole mission along with him. It really had nothing of military importance, nor was it an easy place to land, especially with their dwindling fuel. But it was away from the main defences of Palermo and offered the possibility of escape inland and some sympathetic locals.

One of those locals caught the eye of Fallon.

Alongside the interrogation camp was a housing estate and, when the men were out exercising, local women would walk past and Fallon clearly caught their eye. Their English-speaking guard informed him that one of the girls wanted to speak to him but, as Fallon notes in his memoirs, the guard had told her:

"No — he is a very dangerous man".

So that was the end of that flirtation.

Even in the direst of situations, the irrepressible spirit of men like Fallon is evident in the historical and social artefacts. This spirit was going to be what got them through to the end of the war.

OPPOSITE: TAG L/A Johnny Fallon (Fallon Family).

Pad

60

15
PLAN OF ACTION

"HEAD IN A BOOK AGAIN, CLOG?" Fallon asked, walking the three steps from his bed to Taylor's.

"My notebook," Taylor corrected him gently. "Sketching the rooftops from when we were back in Cefalù. They're different to back home. The tiles seem to pick up the warmth of the light and the angles on the roofs are more gentle, softer, somehow."

"If they're softer, how do we break through them?" Hunt asked, his back pressed against the wooden wall of the hut as he surveyed their tiny room. He'd been pacing the floor like a caged tiger since their arrival, only stopping to sleep or when there were too many men in the room to be able to walk between the beds.

"We don't need to," Denis Kelleher said, looking up from the Monopoly board in front of him. "We just need to find out when the guards change over so we can slip out while they're occupied." Kelleher had already been at the camp when they arrived and had made friends with Campbell at the first handshake.

"Who's going to tell you that? Uncle Tom Cobley?" Hunt asked, his feet twitching as though they were still walking. "And we need to know more than the time of their tea breaks."

"I beg to differ," Kelleher said, ensuring the map was secreted back inside the game before sitting down next to Campbell on a narrow, hard bed. There was a good ten inches in height and width difference between them, making them look like ill-matched bookends. "We keep everything simple. We just walk out, casual as you like, and charm our way home."

"The Italians in Cefalù seemed like good folk," Fallon said. "Especially the young ladies." Fallon tipped his head coquettishly to a chorus of muted wolf whistles.

"We need to come up with something distinctly more robust than that, man"

OPPOSITE: Fragment of painting by Taylor of the PoW camp in Padula, Italy.

said Hunt, his face showing frown lines that hadn't been there a month earlier.

"Papers, that's the first thing we need," Campbell said, ignoring Hunt, his characteristic determination to stay positive still evident. "Money, clothes, chocolate…" He started making an imaginary list in the air. Nothing could be written down. They gave all their paper and pencils to Taylor for his sketches. And no one wanted to be caught with plans for an escape. They'd seen what happened to men who were.

"So where are these supplies coming from?" Hunt asked. "It's not like we've got a NAAFI to make us all a little picnic to take on our adventure, is it?"

"Ah, I've made a friend," Osborn said, a wry smile lighting his face. "There's always someone who isn't quite what they seem. I've been working on that guard who speaks good English. Let's just say he sympathises with our situation." Osborn withdrew a handful of liras from a flap concealed under the collar of his jacket. "He's going to source supplies for us. Seems that Mussolini isn't popular with everyone."

"How's the artwork coming along, Clog?" Robinson asked, peering over his shoulder.

"You tell me," Taylor said, holding up his notebook to show Robinson the concealed forgeries tucked in its pages.

"You've got an eye for detail, I'll give you that," Robinson said, nodding appreciatively at the ID cards created with Taylor's careful handwriting and rubber stamps crafted out of the soles of the boots so generously donated to them by their Italian captors.

"Excellent. Keep at it, Clog. That train line we passed on the way here runs along the coast," Campbell said, now drawing out a route with his finger. "If we can get away from here and find some friendlies, we'll be home in a jiffy."

"I like this idea," Fallon said, joining them on the bunk. "Saturday nights just haven't been the same recently. Can't think why."

"Count me out of this hare-brained idea," Hunt said, jumping to his feet and standing in the doorway. A blast of cold, winter air pushed into the meagre hut as he opened the door.

"Put the wood in the hole," Osborn shouted, not looking up from Campbell's invisible map. The door slammed behind Hunt.

"The CO seems a tad ruffled," Fallon said.

"Can't blame him," Taylor said. "Hal Far must be missing us in the air."

"And the CO never was one to keep his feet on the ground," Campbell said, his own feet firmly planted on the floor while Kelleher's dangled over the edge of the bed. "He likes to keep busy and we're not exactly helping the war effort while we're stuck here."

"It's only a matter of time before they split up the rest of us. God knows what's happened to our Frank and Matty," Taylor said, looking up from his sketchbook. The room fell silent as they sat listening to a fierce easterly wind howling outside.

"Gentlemen," Osborn said, stepping into the middle of the group. "Let's get this plan into action."

14

P.S. I enclose a photostat of two sketches of Marlag Nord which I made in a small sketch book. They might interest you.

From memory I have drawn the plan below to show where the pictures were drawn from. Our Compound was, I suppose, about 250 yards long × 100 yards wide overall
RWT

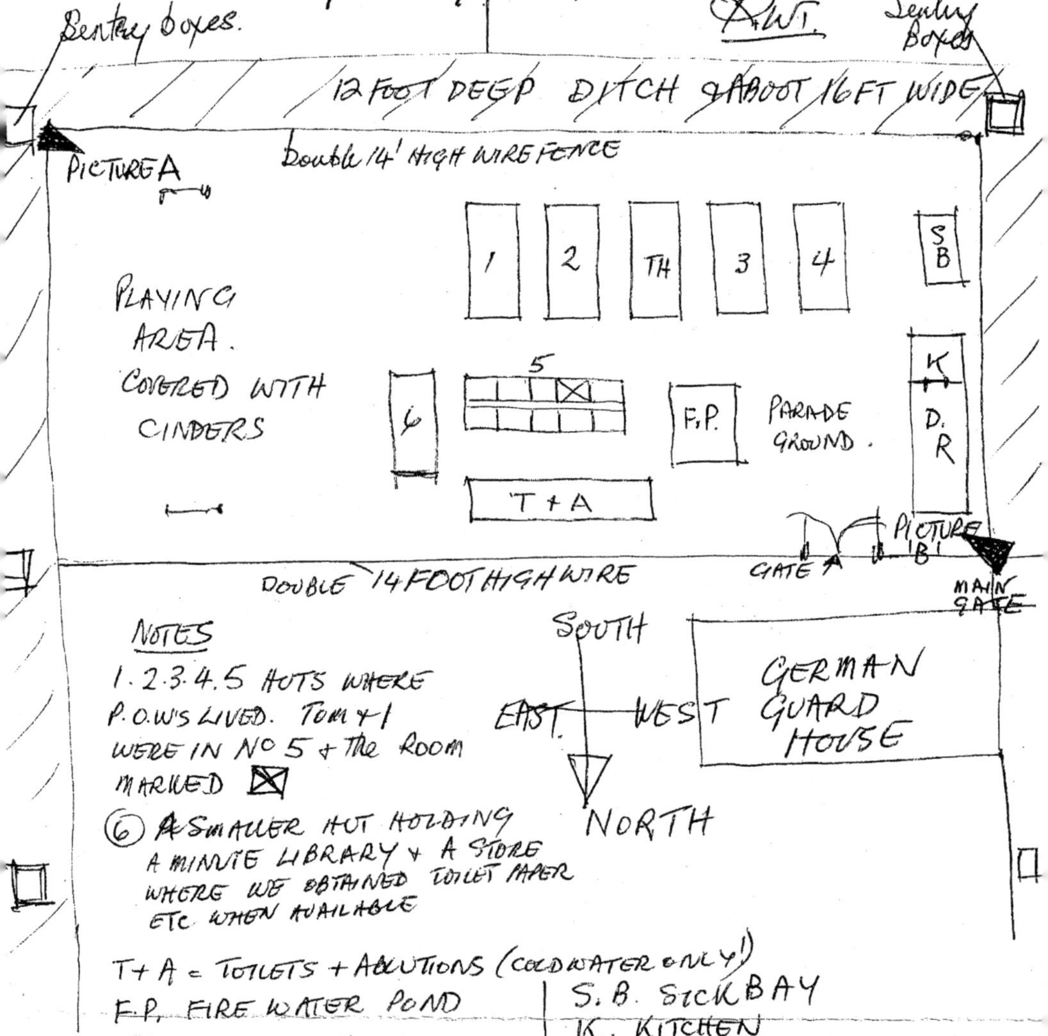

Sentry boxes.

Sentry Boxes

12 FOOT DEEP DITCH (ABOUT 16FT WIDE)

PICTURE A

Double 14' HIGH WIRE FENCE

| 1 | 2 | TH | 3 | 4 | S B |

PLAYING AREA.
COVERED WITH CINDERS

5 ⊠

6

F.P.

PARADE GROUND.

K
D. R

T + A

DOUBLE 14 FOOT HIGH WIRE

GATE

PICTURE 'B'

MAIN GATE

NOTES

1. 2. 3. 4. 5 HUTS WHERE P.O.W's LIVED. TOM + I WERE IN No 5 + the ROOM MARKED ⊠

⑥ A SMALLER HUT HOLDING A MINUTE LIBRARY + A STORE WHERE WE OBTAINED TOILET PAPER ETC WHEN AVAILABLE

SOUTH

EAST — WEST

NORTH

GERMAN GUARD HOUSE

T + A = TOILETS + ABLUTIONS (COLD WATER ONLY!)
F.P. FIRE WATER POND
TH. THEATRE HUT

S. B. SICK BAY
K. KITCHEN
D.R. DINING ROOM

16
SET A COURSE FOR HOME

CAMPBELL, FALLON, HUNT, PARKE, Osborn, Robinson, and Taylor were taken to PoW camps in Italy, Poland and Germany. From the moment they were imprisoned, they were planning their escape and, for two of them, executing those plans. Where their original mission had failed, they simply moved on to a new mission: finding their way home.

In autumn 1943, Fallon didn't so much escape 41 Italian PoW Camp Montalbo as stroll out. Like many other prisoners, he took advantage of the collapse of the Italian military when Mussolini was deposed after the Allied troops took Sicily. Fallon simply walked away from the camp, living off what he could scavenge in the countryside for six weeks. But with winter approaching, no way of knowing what was happening in the world and starving slowly, he had to risk asking for help. He struck lucky. He found a farmhouse and a wonderful Italian family who fed and protected him for almost a year. Whenever the Germans arrived in the area, the farmer would hide him under the floorboards of the farmhouse, along with the dust and the mice. Fallon never much liked mice after that.

Breakfast was always a meagre affair for the farming family, living off what they could grow and the tiny rations they received. But they were generous, sharing food and clothes with him and, as Fallon sat enjoying a little bread and warm milk one morning, there was a fierce shout and the door burst open. A team of British commandos, weapons levelled, spilled into the kitchen.

"I'm English," Fallon shouted, raising his hands. "And these fine people are our allies."

The commandos spotted an opportunity. They took Fallon with them as their radio operator. They had a mission to complete, and he was usefully dressed as a

---

OPPOSITE: Sketch representing Marlag Nord POW camp, Germany. Included in a letter that RW Taylor wrote in March 1994 to Debbie McLister, the widow of a former POW whom he shared a room with at Marlag Nord.

civilian, had much sought after radio skills and undeniable calm in the face of the enemy. Fallon jumped at the chance to tag along, knowing that if they were caught they would all have been executed (as it was German military procedure to execute all captured commandos). With their secret mission successfully completed, he was flown back to England in September 1944. He arrived in Wigan and promptly bumped into a neighbour who greeted him with, "Hello Jack — long time, no see. Have you been away?" Such was the understated welcome home for many a soldier.

Campbell had quite the Boys' Own adventure after ditching in Cefalù that night. Although initially imprisoned together, the men of 830 Squadron were progressively split up, a common tactic to breakdown morale and cohesion. Campbell was sent to Stalag III where he and Lieutenant Denis Kelleher, aged twenty-five, became lifelong friends and hatched a plan to escape. Because of their disparity in height and stature, they were known as "the long and tall of it" while they were in the PoW camp. Together, they learned German, watched the movements of the guards, worked out that Bremen was the nearest railway station and, one night in 1943, simply walked out of the camp into the mist. Using the scraps of German they had learned in the various PoW camps, they set about passing themselves off as Merchant Service officers. On the road towards Bremen, their feet already sore from walking and their fitness questionable after years of imprisonment, they met an old woman and their first chance to try out their budding linguistic abilities.

"Guten Abend, gnädige Frau, ist das die Straße nach Bremen?" Campbell asked, in halting German and turning on the biggest of smiles.

"Ja ja. Folgen Sie dieser Straße geradeaus nach Bremen hinein," she replied, anxiously stepping away from them. "Es ist eine dunkle Nacht, um spazieren zu gehen."

"Ja. Sehr gut. Danke, schönen," Kelleher said, keen to try a little German and not really understanding what the woman had said. "Abend noch."

"Ja, danke…" she said, watching the two strange men cautiously as they walked away from her.

Their first test accomplished, they walked through the night, on to Bremen. Early next morning, tired and thirsty, they arrived to find a city that had survived the war well. There were few signs of damage and the locals were going about business with an air of normality. Both men craved coffee and a rest but had failed to consider that they needed ration coupons to buy anything so luxurious. They had to make do with disappearing into the crowds of Bremen station and another test of their German: buying tickets.

The ticket office clerk barely looked up as they handed over some of their precious Deutschmarks, sourced through the kindness of guards who no longer believed in the words of the Führer. Their hours of playing seemingly innocuous board games and practising German in their prison huts were also paying off. Their edition of Monopoly had contained ingeniously hidden maps and instructions, never spotted by their captors, and learning German was actively encouraged. Boarding the crowded train, they were forced to stand in the corridor while Gestapo officers checked papers. It took all their nerve and bravado to stand still and wait as their tickets and papers were checked. Just as they were handing them back, a shout went up from another officer as he hauled a young German soldier to his feet. There was an error on his papers and the Gestapo officer was going to make sure everyone on the train heard what happened when you didn't have the right papers. Campbell and Kelleher held fast and watched, their hearts pounding like ack-ack guns.

For three days, they travelled through Germany, walking until their feet were swollen, catching busy trains and hoping their false papers wouldn't be discovered, occasionally drinking beer, and chatting to German policemen. At one point, a very helpful police officer who was struggling to understand their faulty German called for backup from a colleague – because he spoke Dutch! By now, they had

OPPOSITE: Sub-Lieutenant Stewart Campbell (Campbell Family).

eaten the little chocolate that they had brought with them from the camp and were desperately tired and hungry. In all, it took them twenty-two days to find their way back to England. On arriving home, Campbell walked into his parents' house and asked, "Hello folks. How's the war?" Both Campbell and Kelleher were awarded the MBE and Campbell went on to do test flying with the Armoured Trials and Development Unit (ATDU) Unit before joining 811 Mosquito Squadron at the end of the war.

Woozle Osborn went on to have an illustrious career. After failing to escape the PoW camps, he returned home and went straight into the pay of the British Government's Secret Intelligence Service, MI6. Dorril describes how he was employed by MI6 in Asia, tackling communist infiltration whilst working for the British government under a subterfuge that compromised the Colombo Plan study programme and its development mission. Osborn became an expert in counterinsurgency warfare, his knowledge gained during the Malayan Emergency. This work taught him the importance of "hearts and minds" in winning the allegiance of local people when he became a hill tribes adviser in Laos. His time there is noted in records as giving "valuable service to the Laotian government," but there is little more detail. We can only surmise that he worked covertly in extreme

ABOVE: Sub-Lt Taylor's logbook entry, 11th Nov 1941. Torpedo Roam. Landed Sicilian Coast. Cefalù. Flight time: 7 hours (Taylor Family).

situations, negotiating relationships that led to the exchange of critical intelligence in this protracted conflict. The clue to the nature of his role is that he disappeared without a trace during his time in Laos and emerged with an OBE.

Other memoirs and histories of this period fail to mention Osborn: a sure sign that his work was remarkable and of high value. It's likely that Osborn's unique experience with short-take-off-and-landing (STOL) aircraft, learned on aircraft carriers, gave him the expertise needed to train Hmong pilots for the Royal Lao Air Force. Their battles against the Pathet Lao and North Vietnamese regular forces were some of the bloodiest of the conflict and decimated their communities. Osborn's "hearts and minds" work would have been crucial to sustaining their engagement with such heavy losses.

Osborn's obituary in The Times, dated 12 May 1997, indicated that he was in Laos for seven years, until he suffered a series of strokes and retired to Spain in 1971. Throughout his life, it seems that Woozle was unconventional and not afraid to challenge the status quo. His obituary noted that his "undiplomatically boozy parties in Vientiane were legendary." Perhaps his disagreement with Hunt, the CO, was an indication of where his career was going to take him and the kind of maverick spirit that would drive his life.

Taylor remained as a PoW until the end of the war, making sketches of the buildings around him and notes about his life as a prisoner. The Red Cross managed to send books on architecture into the camp for him. He devoured them, pouring over the detail and learning as much as he could in the stark conditions. After the war he put the efforts of the Red Cross to good use and graduated from Oxford as an architect. With a new career in sight, Taylor married and started a family before emigrating to Christchurch in New Zealand in the 1950s.

Hunt was the oldest man on the mission at thirty-five and was already married with three children before he became a PoW. During his early military career, he had studied French, but this was of no use to him when he was held in either the Italian PoW Camp number 35, Certosa di Padula Monastery, near Salerno until 1945 or the German PoW Camp Marlag und Milag Nord, Westertimke (Tarmstedt). Following the war, he remained in the Royal Navy and, in 1951, his aunt, Katherine Julia Hunt, left him £1,500 in her will "as some compensation for the hardships suffered by him as a prisoner of war." The recognition of how much these men sacrificed was felt keenly by both those who had served and civilians for many years after the war ended. Hunt died on 9th November 1981 in Southbourne, West Sussex, aged seventy-six.

We know that Griffiths' family in 1941 had no idea what happened to him and held out hope that he had been captured but somehow had lost his memory. His brother, Gwilym, kept looking for him throughout the war and wrote home in 1943, describing a football match between soldiers, Scotland vs Wales, played in Libya. This match took place just before Gwilym moved on to fight in Italy where he penned the letter shown opposite.

Robinson remained in a PoW camp in Poland until the end of the war. Even though he was a captive he was made a Full (Temporary) Lieutenant in 1943, indicating that his leadership skills shone through the worst of situations. On his release from the PoW camp in 1945, his thirst for a challenge was quick to surface again. He boarded RMS Orion on May 1945 on a journey to Tasmania. On his travels, and working as an engineer, he met a nurse, Suzette Stokes, and moved to Perth, Australia. They were married for forty-seven years but did not have children. Robinson was another of the crew in search of new adventures and not afraid to find them in a very different country. We know little of his story as a civilian as he did not leave any memoirs or direct descendants. He died at eighty-nine years of age.

ABOVE: Lieutenant-Commander John Gunthorpe Hunt on his wedding day in 1932 at the Holy Trinity Church in Sliema, Malta.

Parke spent more than three years as a PoW in Sulmona, Italy, where he met Graham McInnes, an RAF Officer, and struck up a firm friendship. With the war over, they is looking forward to the time when the 'Bury will be playing once more. I wonder if you will be in the team, Ralph? I don't see why not, and also Derrick too! Maybe Glyn also will come along for he tells me he gets plenty of football up north. Ken would most certainly have played with us but for this damned war which has messed everything up. If it's possible to find him, I will. At least I'm going in the right direction to do so!! I'd really feel that my coming out here had been worth it if I did find him. We shall see. I hope Nancy is keeping well these days, and Derrick putting on the weight he'll need if he is going to turn out with us. Have you had a holiday? If so, write and tell me of it. Mother, Gladys and Sylvia, I see have returned from a splendid time in N. Wales. Lucky people. Still, North Africa isn't too bad once one gets used to the heat, flies, sand, disease and bad smells! This usually takes a while, they tell me the first two years are the worst out here! Anyway, drop me a line, you too Derrick. You don't know how bucked I feel to hear from you all. So cheerio for now, wish me luck.

Yours, Gwil

were liberated from the PoW camp and both set about enjoying some of the freedoms that had been missing, living the lives of carefree young men who liked an adventure. Parke became a Warrant Officer and, after a year back on English soil, his PoW pal suggested a trip out on his motorbike. Friendships made in those camps moulded the lives on the men forever. Also on the motorbike was another RAF Warrant Officer and the three of them set off from Bramcote Aerodrome. Their journey was short. They failed to take a bend and were catapulted into a ditch. All three of them died in that accident. Parke was only twenty-six years old, a young man who had seen considerable action and had been awarded the Distinguished Service Medal for those missions over the Mediterranean with 830 Squadron Royal Navy.

ABOVE: Brothers Gwilym Griffiths (left) and Ken Griffiths (right).
OPPOSITE: Registry showing the location of Matthew Parke's grave.

ARKE, Wt. Offr. MATTHEW, 543666, D.S.M.
A.F. 7th July, 1946. Age 26. Son of Joseph C.
arke and Mary Parke, of Ballymagroarty. Sec. S.
ass A. Grave 153.

ATERSON, S.B.A. JOHN ARCHIBALD, V/88925.
.C.N.V.R. H.M.C.S. *Leaside*. 8th May, 1945.
ge 19. Son of Frank C. Paterson and Eva L.
aterson, of Peterborough, Ontario, Canada.
. of E. Plot. Sec. F. Grave 49.

ORTER, Seaman GEORGE WILLIAM, LT/JX.
3707. R.N. Patrol Service. H.M. Drifter *Pax*.
th August, 1941. Age 27. Son of George and
sther Porter, of Pelaw, Gateshead, Co. Durham.
. of E. Plot. Sec. F. Grave 11.

UINN, P.O. JAMES PATRICK, P/5509D. R.N.R.
.M.S. *La Malouine*. 5th November, 1940. Age
. Son of James Henry and Elizabeth Quinn, of
nderland, Co. Durham ; husband of Eliza
uinn, of Sunderland. R.C. Plot. Sec. M. Grave 1.

AYNOR, E.R.A. 4th Cl. WILLIAM PETER FRANK,
/MX. 61634. R.N. H.M.S. *Roxborough*. 8th
ay, 1941. Age 23. Son of William Peter Raynor
d of Letitia Agnes Raynor (*née* Reid) ; husband
' Margaret Roberta Raynor, of Heamoor, Pen-
nce, Cornwall. C. of E. Plot. Sec. F. Grave 7.

EDMAN, Seaman, EDWARD, P/X. 9910. R.N.R.
.M.S. *Victory*. 25th March, 1941. Age 36.
n of William and Elizabeth Redman, of Sunder-
nd, Co. Durham ; husband of Lavinia Hannah
edman, of Sunderland. C. of E. Plot. Sec. F.
rave 3.

EE, L. Bdr. JOHN A., 1078008. 547 Coast Regt.,
oyal Artillery. 15th June, 1941. Age 22. Son
' Robert J. Ree and Isabel Ree, of Londonderry.
c. S. Class B. Grave 850.I.

ODGERS, Sgt. WILLIAM, 527615. R.A.F. 27th
arch, 1945. Age 28. Son of Robert William and
ary Jane Rodgers ; husband of Beulah Edna
odgers, of Londonderry. Sec. S. Class B. Grave
06.D.

OSE, P.O. Steward CHARLES FREDERICK, P/L.
976. R.N. H.M.S. *Banff*. 26th July, 1942.
ge 39. Son of Charles and Rose Emma Rose ;
sband of Lorna Irene Rose, of Southsea,
ampshire. C. of E. Plot. Sec. 7. Grave 25.

ROWE, A.B. ROBERT, C/J. 29614. R.N. H.M.S. LONDON-
Redmill. 27th April, 1945. Age 47. Husband of DERRY CITY
Rachel Florence Rowe, of St. Pancras, London. CEMETERY
C. of E. Plot. Sec. F. Grave 48.   U.K. 7313

RUFFELL, Fus. CHARLES WILLIAM, 6980547.
2nd Bn. The Royal Inniskilling Fusiliers. 30th
April, 1941. Age 18. Son of Charles William and
Grace Ruffell, of Londonderry. Sec. N. Class B.
Grave 635.

SAMPSON, Lieut. RICHARD JOHN (DICK), R.N.V.R.
H.M.S. *Broadwater*. 19th October, 1941. Age 32.
Son of Mr. and Mrs. G. Sampson, of Slough,
Buckinghamshire. C. of E. Plot. Sec. F. Grave 14.

SANDREY, Ord. Sigmn. LLEWELLYN, D/SSX.
33876. R.N. H.M.S. *Broadwater*. 19th October,
1941. C. of E. Plot. Sec. F. Grave 19.

SCALES, Ord. Sea. ALFRED E., V/10996.
R.C.N.V.R. H.M.C.S. *Collingwood*. 5th May,
1943. Age 18. Son of Mrs. M. J. Scales, of
Regina, Saskatchewan, Canada. C. of E. Plot.
Sec. F. Grave 36.

SIMMS, Cpl. MATTHEW, 6977189. The Royal
Irish Fusiliers. 11th September, 1940. Sec. M.
Class D. Grave 1351.

SOMERSET, Apprentice ARTHUR, Merchant
Navy. M.V. *Oilfield* (Newcastle). 28th April,
1941. Age 18. Son of John and Henrietta Somerset, of East Hoathly, Sussex. Sec. S. Class B.
Grave 1216.

TAYLOR, Pte. REGINALD, 4387696. 1st Bn. The
Green Howards (Yorkshire Regt.). 15th May,
1941. Age 27. Son of William and Catherine
Taylor, of Brompton-on-Swale, Yorkshire. R.C.
Plot. Sec. M. Grave 3.

TOMLINSON, Stores Asst. FRANK, P/MX.
751814. R.N. H.M.L.S.T. 3515. 4th May, 1946.
Age 19. Son of James and Jessie Tomlinson, of
Woolton, Liverpool. C. of E. Plot. Sec. F. Grave
51.

WALSHAW, L. Cpl. LAWRENCE RAYMOND,
T/117119. 5 Div. Ammunition Coy., R.A.S.C.
25th June, 1941. C. of E. Plot. Sec. F. Grave 9.

51

17
THE MEMORIAL SERVICE

THIS SHORT HISTORY WAS THE STORY of one mission where weather, navigation, technology, fuel, leadership, and exceptional skill all played a part. Factors that still influence the way pilots and crew operate today.

It is also the story of one pilot's search to bring history to life and people together. Luca Lazzara traced the ancestors of the men of 830 Squadron, the men who arrived so unexpectedly in his hometown of Cefalù long before he was born or took to the skies himself. As a pilot, he was drawn to their story and a desire to commemorate the lost aircrew. Luca found all but two of the men's families and has built up lasting friendships with the ancestors he has met.

On 13th October 2019, Luca hosted a memorial service in Cefalù for the nine crew members of 830 Squadron. As a pilot operating in a very different time and place, he had been drawn to the image of the Swordfish and the story of the men who had been forced to land on the beach and at sea, something all pilots are trained to do and trained to avoid.

Sub-Lieutenant Raymond Warren "Clog" Taylor's family have been actively involved in the research to inform this book and the artwork of his daughter, Sally, is included in these pages showing her own affection for the legendary Stringbag. Eighteen members of his extended family came from New Zealand to the Memorial in Cefalù to visit Clog's landing site.

Sub-Lieutenant Stewart Campbell's family, including his daughter, Linda, attended the Memorial Ceremony. We are particularly grateful to his son, Ian, for the excellent source material he has made available to us through his own website and his support for our research.

Lieutenant George Myles "Woozle" Osborn lived until he was eighty-two years old and led the most extraordinary of lives. We have been in contact with a

OPPOSITE: Memorial service, Cefalù, 13th October 2019. Sally Ogilvie, (left), Luca Lazzara (centre), John Taylor (right).

cousin (a former Australian Royal Navy Officer) and his grandchildren.

Leading Airman Johnny Fallon's son, Chris, attended the Memorial Ceremony and has generously supported us with access to his father's personal memoirs.

Cefalù looked beautiful on the day of the Memorial Ceremony. Warm autumn sunshine welcomed the visitors and local people showed the famous hospitality that the aircrew had commented on in their own memoirs. Giovanni, the owner of the old "Cinema Di Francesca" in the town had helped Luca to organise the ceremony and greeted the families like long-lost friends. Luca took the visitors past the Cathedral and tourist attractions down to the seafront, to see Taylor's landing site. This was quite a moment for Sally and her family; the place her father had executed that exceptional touchdown. Using his research and the maps from Professor Purpura, Luca was also able to show the group where Campbell and Fallon had ditched at sea and then the visitors retraced their escape across the beach and up the hill, towards the railway line. Unlike Campbell and Fallon, the visitors weren't captured at gunpoint! Instead, they were treated to lunch at the *Baglio del Falco* restaurant where the owner has two framed pictures of Taylor's plane displayed proudly on the wall. It was an afternoon of reminiscing, laughter and friendship as the Taylor family shared a book they had created full of Luca's research on the mission, a copy of Clog Taylor's logbook and, presented by his grandson, Jimmy, a model kit for Luca to build his own Swordfish.

On the following day, the Memorial Service, hosted by the Cefalù authorities and the Mayor, took place accompanied by a small air display with microlights from the local airfield. The Ceremony ended at the beach, where Luca's search had started. A memorial board was unveiled in honour of the men who found themselves in enemy skies with no way home.

These fragments of military and social history are being lost to us, like the Swordfish, sinking beneath the surface. Time means fewer of the men and women of the Second World War remain alive to give us their first-hand accounts of what really happened. We can do no less than remember them.

OPPOSITE: Poster for the memorial ceremony, 13 October 2019. The translation of the title is "A Story of Airplanes, Pilots and Men."

Cefalù

Comune di Cefalù

Cefalu

13 ottobre 2019

1 NOVEMBRE 1941
toria di aerei, piloti e uomini

Uno degli Swordfish inglesi sul Lungomare di Cefalù - Foto archivio Giovanni Marino

la consiliare

00 Incontro con i familiari del sottotenente pilota
R. W. Taylor e del mitragliere telegrafista J. Fallon

Inaugurazione mostra fotografica

Interverranno: Rosario Lapunzina, *Sindaco di Cefalù*
Giovanni Iuppa, *Presidente del Consiglio Comunale*,
Giovanni Cristina, Luca Lazzara, Giuseppe Martino,
Serge Rajmondi, Gianfranco Purpora

00 *Break*

Lungomare Giardina

15.30 Esibizione aerea del
Volo Club Albatros
di Termini Imerese

16.00 Traversata in barca
dal Molo al Lungomare

16.30 Scopertura della
epigrafe commemorativa

Cefalù 13 Ottobre 2019

Epilogue

AS WITH ALL HISTORIES, we know more about some people than others and we would welcome your help to fill in gaps and tell us your own stories.

In 2019, Luca brought together the family members he had been able to trace to give the men of the Swordfish mission the memorial they deserved. Luca grew up in Cefalù and dreamed of becoming a pilot and is now a Captain with Malta Air, an airline based where this story started. Thankfully, it didn't take a war to achieve his goal and, as a pilot, he understood the skill and courage needed to land a plane in such impossible conditions. His insatiable curiosity brought this story to life and the families of the crew together for the first time. As an Italian living in England, he had an acute sense of the importance of a shared European history.

But there are still some details missing and this is where we'd like your help. We want to find out more about the men and their families for whom we have few details and to add to the rapidly dwindling sources of history from this period. If you have any more pieces of the puzzle, please contact us as we are continuing to research other lost men, submarines, and aircraft.

Robinson and Parke are the men we would like to know more about; Parke because he died young, Robinson because he did not have children. These men would certainly have had friends and colleagues who have descendants so we would welcome any information to add to the history, and the future, that the crew of the Stringbags left for us.

And we would like you to share any photos or fragments of military history that you feel are worthy of research. These stories provide us with a better understanding of the experiences and bravery of the men and women of previous conflicts. We would like to find as many of these untold stories as possible, to save them for future historians. Contact us at swordfish@doubledagger.ca.

_____

Opposite: 80 years later…Luca Lazzara landing in Sicily in a 737 (Lazzara, 2021).

SOURCES

Armoured Aircraft Carriers in World War II. Operation Judgement 2023 https://www.armouredcarriers.com/operation-judgement-swordfish-attack-taranto-from-hms-illustrious

Bach, R. W. Collaboration of Britain, Australia and New Zealand in the Second Indochina War, with Particular Focus on Laos, 1952-1975. MPhil. Thesis, University of Queensland, Australia. 2016

BBC, WW2 People's War: 830 Squadron, Fleet Air Arm, Malta. An archive of World War Two memories – written by the public, gathered by the BBC, 2005 https://www.bbc.co.uk/history/ww2peopleswar/stories/19/a4029419.shtml.

BBC Scotland, Veteran Pilot John Moffat Recalls Sinking the Bismarck. Aired 13th December, 2006 on the BBC. https://www.bbc.co.uk/news/av/uk-scotland-38303674

Beadell, S. J. (Lieutenant), Royal Navy official photographer, public domain images via Wikimedia Commons 2022.

Bragadin, M. A. (1957) The Italian Navy in World War II. United States Naval Institute

Campbell, I. 830 Squadron [online] 2012. http://iancampbells.com/830squadron/LF2.html

Dorril, S. MI6: Fifty Years of Special Operations. Fourth Estate. 2001

Dorril, S. MI6: Inside the Covert World of Her Majesty's Secret Intelligence Service. New York: Simon & Schuster. 2002.

Fallon, C. email to Lazzara, L. 13/3/18, sharing details of Johnny Fallon's memoir.

Fleet Air Arm, Malta War Diary: story of a George Cross 1941 https://maltagc70.

Opposite: A view of Swordfish HS235 "Q" of No. 1 Naval Gunnery Air Gunnery School (LAC).

wordpress.com/2021/11/12/12-november-1941-air-war-losses-and-gains/

Glover, P. Email containing research on Swordfish V4295(5L) February to November 1941. 2021

Guntharp, J. Topics in Radio Technology, Applications, Techniques and Countermeasures in WWII and Early Cold War. eBookIt.com 2019

Historic Gosport, Gosport Tube, 2022 https://historicgosport.uk/gosport-tube/

Horan, M. (With Gallantry and Determination, 1998. Available at https://www.kbismarck.com/article2.html

ICAO, HF Guidance Materials [online]. 2015. Available at https://www.icao.int/EURNAT/EUR%20and%20NAT%20Documents/NAT%20Documents/NAT%20Documents/NAT%20Doc%20003/NAT%20Doc003%20-%20HF%20Guidance%20v3.0.0_2015.pdf

Kennedy, L, The Sinking of the Bismark (p.142-145-146), 1974, quoted in Lazzara, L. and Purpura, G. Il "Pescespada" di Cefalù e l'affondamento della Bismarck, 2021

Klein, C. Remembering the sinking of the Bismarck, 2016. https://www.history.com/news/remembering-the-sinking-of-the-bismarck

Lamb, C, War in a Stringbag. London: Cassell Military Paperbacks, 2001 edition.

Lazzara, L, Message left on WW2Talk, 2016. http://www.ww2talk.com/index.php?threads/fleet-air-arm-830th-squadron-malta.68291/#post-734973_

Lazzara, L, Memorial Day on Cefalù, YouTube, 2019. - here https://www.youtube.com/watch?v=uNXeJnCLxgw&t=1109s

Lawson, D. Email to L Lazzara, 2021

Lettens. Figure 1, The Bismarck underwater. 2009. Available at https://www.wrecksite.eu/docbrowser.aspx?87

Marcon, T. Storia Militare: Abbattuti dallo Scirocco [online]. 1998. Available at http://www1.unipa.it/dipstdir/portale/ARTICOLI%20PURPURA/links%20archeologici/Abbattuti%20dal%20vento%20di%20scirocco%20ridotto.pdf

Osborn, R. Obituaries in "Slipstream", 1997. https://www.faaaa.asn.au/wp-content/uploads/2016/08/Slipstream-Vol-8-3-Oct97.pdf

Poolman, K. Night Strike from Malta, Jane's Publishing Company: London, 1980.

Sturtivant, R Burrow, M. Fleet Air Arm aircrafts 1939 to 1945, Air Britain Historians Ltd; First Edition. 1 Aug. 1995.

The Scotsman. Appreciation: Robert Lawson [online], 2010. Available at https://www.scotsman.com/news/obituaries/appreciation-robert-lawson-2442474

Smith-Barry, R.R. NOTES ON TEACHING FLYING: Instructor's Courses at No.1 Training Squadron, Gosport. Part I, 1917.

Spooner, T. Faith, Hope and Malta GC. Swindon, Newton Publishers, 1992.

The Telegraph. Lt-Cdr Lawson, 2010. Available at https://www.telegraph.co.uk/news/obituaries/military-obituaries/naval-obituaries/7720761/LtLieutenant-Cdr-Bobby-Lawson.html

Steel, D. Ludovic Kennedy Obituary [online], 2009. Available at https://www.theguardian.com/media/2009/oct/19/sir-ludovic-kennedy-obituary

Unknown, "£1,500 for ex-P.O.W." Eastbourne Gazette August 8th, 1951.

FOLLOWING PAGES:

Pages 84-85. A water colour painting of a Fairey Swordfish by "Clog" Taylor's daughter, Sally.
Pages 86-87. Fairey Swordfish NF 370, fitted with an ASV Mk X beneath the nose, on display at IWM Duxford. (Alan Wilson)
Pages 88-89. Swordfish W5856, the oldest surviving airworthy Swordfish in the world, shown flying at the 2016 Farnborough Airshow. As part of the Navy Wings collection, funded by the Fly Navy Heritage Trust, the aircraft is shown here in the livery of 820 Naval Air Squadron as it was during the attack that sunk the Bismarck in 1941. (Oren Rozen)

The Fairey Swordfish

ST

ABOVE: Ray "Clog" Taylor still flying on his 80th birthday in 1988, in a Tiger Moth. (Taylor Family)

ABOVE: Aircrew across the divide: Ray Taylor's logbook and Luca Lazzara's Captain's stripes.

DOUBLE‡DAGGER
— www.doubledagger.ca —

Double Dagger Books is Canada's only military-focused publisher. Conflict and warfare have shaped human history since before we began to record it. The earliest stories that we know of, passed on as oral tradition, speak of war, and more importantly, the essential elements of the human condition that are revealed under its pressure.

We are dedicated to publishing material that, while rooted in conflict, transcend the idea of "war" as merely a genre. Fiction, non-fiction, and stuff that defies categorization, we want to read it all.

Because if you want peace, study war.

ABOUT THE AUTHOR

Captain Luca Lazzara is a 737 pilot for a major European airline based in Italy and he has a passion for making connections between people and stories. With over 10,000 hours and more than 200 different airports in his logbook, spread across two decades in the aviation industry, Luca loves flying passengers across Europe, North Africa and the Middle East, something he dreamed of since he was a child.

While he was still living in the UK, he discovered the photograph online of the Swordfish that inspired this book, and his research on 'The lost Bismarck Swordfish' hit the headlines both in the UK and Italy in 2021 on the 80th Anniversary of the sinking of the famous German battleship. His work means that he often traces the flight paths of many of those courageous aviators, giving him a unique connection between the past and present.

Originally from the picturesque town of Cefalù on the north coast of Sicily, his hometown is the focus for the story of the Swordfish mission. Luca initially trained to design yachts and holds a Bachelor of Arts degree in International Business, specialising in aviation, and is now coaching and training others in the industry.

ABOUT THE AUTHOR

Inspired by the voices of extraordinary people in extreme situations, **Bev Morris** writes through listening to stories told by survivors. From women survivors of abuse to soldiers at war, from people to places, she is drawn to experiences that question the very nature of humans and our impact on the world and each other. She seeks out the fragments of trauma that lodge themselves deep inside ordinary people, changing them forever, sometimes for the better. Often for the worse.

Bev's work itself is created in fragments; poems, flash fiction, haiku, micro-scripts. She looks to give a space to unheard voices, even when these voices falter or scream.

Bev's first military history, 'An Average Pilot', is being published by Double Dagger Books, and her wellbeing book, 'Moments of Joy', is self-published by Marvellous Minds Creatives. Her poetry is published by the award-winning Beautiful Dragons (Ragged Rocks, Running Rascals, Bloody Amazing, Lighting Out, Watch the Birdie, Noble Dissent, Well, Dam!, Not a Drop) and her flash fiction is published by Retreat West (The Perfect Word) and Writers Online (The Show at the End of the Pier).

As well as performing eco-poetry as part of Poets 4 the Planet, her eco-article has been published by AMED (The Fifth Element) and her plays (Vagina Blogs, and 9 Lives, 8 Deaths) have been performed by Contexture Theatre. She mentors other writers and storytellers to find their own voice, running writing workshops and groups.

Manufactured by Amazon.ca
Bolton, ON

35492364R00059